"H. Byron Ballard has written a completely [ ] reconnect Pagans with the land and the Wheel of the Year. Part lyrical philosophy, part guidebook, and part instruction manual, *Seasons of a Magical Life* will stay with you long after you have read it." —Deborah Blake, author of *Everyday Witchcraft*

"The gentle art of engaging with the everyday through time and space is wonderfully gathered up here by Ballard, showing us how we can reconnect with the continuity of ancestral life through our own daily actions. Sheer magic." —Caitlín Matthews, author of *Singing the Soul Back Home* and *Diary of a Soul Doctor*

"In today's quest for authenticity and elder wisdom, we are blessed to have the wise voice of one of the most authentic witches I know: Byron Ballard. By authentic, I mean someone who is truly living it and willing to share the hard-won wisdom of her life. Ballard practices all that she teaches, living the magical life with the land she loves and spreading the love of that land wherever she travels to inspire us to love our land. As the proverbial Village Witch, she weaves the strands of poetry, science, history, farming, medicine, and magic into her holistic vision." —Christopher Penczak, cofounder of *The Temple of Witchcraft* and author of *The Plant Spirit Familiar, Spirit Allies,* and *Sons of the Goddess*

"Our world needs elders speaking their truth and sharing their wisdom teachings. Ballard is such a global elder, unafraid of using her voice. *Seasons of a Magical Life* demonstrates an earth-based spirituality that seamlessly weaves together land and soul, building fences and seeking solidarity, tending bees or chickens, and the chore of laundry as a meditative practice. A truly great piece of advice I once received is "Don't get mad, get curious!" This book takes that concept to a new level and demonstrates how preserving the profound innate curiosity of a child can lead us to a life of meaning and authenticity—even when a pandemic rages and challenges all previously held assumptions! Brava!" —Imelda Almqvist, author of *Natural Born Shamans, Medicine of the Imagination,* and *Sacred Art*

"A cozy stroll through H. Byron Ballard's forest-farm, *Seasons of a Magical Life* offers inspiration for a down-home, yet revolutionary, Pagan, animist path." —Christine Grace, author of *The Witch at the Forest's Edge*

"This deeply personal work may be Ballard's best yet. Her words hum quietly from the page, puttering in her garden or decorating for the holidays, but then settle into you like a shot of bourbon. In sharing the seasonal movements of her own corner of the world (and she makes you long to live among the forests of the Smokies with every page), Ballard reconnects the reader with their own lands, spirits, sunshine, and storms. There are reminiscences and recipes, and the philosophical blends seamlessly with the practical as she takes you juneberry picking or teaches you the hidden history of her homeland. She builds upon both magical lore and regional animism and is as likely to lead you down paths of biodiversity and permaculture as altars and charms. In so many ways, *Seasons of a Magical Life* is that 'still, small voice' that goes beyond religion and into the realm of spirit, of nature, and of what it means to be a magical human animal in a living and enchanted world." —Cory Thomas Hutcheson, author of *New World Witchery*

Seasons *of a* Magical Life

A PAGAN PATH OF LIVING

H. Byron Ballard

foreword by Amy Blackthorn

WEISER BOOKS

This edition first published in 2021 by Weiser Books, an imprint of
Red Wheel/Weiser, LLC
With offices at:
65 Parker Street, Suite 7
Newburyport, MA 01950
www.redwheelweiser.com

ISBN: 978-1-57863-723-2
Library of Congress Cataloging-in-Publication Data available upon request.

Cover design by Kathryn Sky-Peck
Cover photograph © by Iuliia Kandaurova/iStock.com
Interior by Ellen Varitimos
Typeset in Centaur

Printed in the United States of America
IBI

10 9 8 7 6 5 4 3 2 I

Every step forward brings us closer to home.
—Casimira Davie

This book is dedicated to the ragtag army of miscreants who are making soil from kitchen scraps, stepping through the borderlands and into terrible realms, speaking from impossible visions, and building new worlds from the rubble of the Tower. You are my beloved kindred and our only real hope.

Contents

PART THREE
HEARTH

Acknowledgments

The idea for this book was suggested by two acolytes of homeliness—Melissa D'Ortensio and Maiasaura WinterHeart—as well as the ongoing work of Dr. Sharon Blackie, which feels like a reunion as well as a revelation (especially her soul-breaking sojourn in the sacred harshness of western Ireland). Dr. Martin Shaw's exquisite work in modern animism inspires and confounds me. To these earth-dirtied souls I owe my thanks. And to these humble and divine beings, Paul Stamets, Paul Strauss, Amanda Strawderman, Bob and Lucia White, Lauri Newman, Jacqueline Honeybee-Durban, Jen Rue, Leann Ticknor, Julie and Sam Thompson, Paul Patton, Amber Shehan, Charlene Suggs, AC. Stauble, and Isaac Alexander Salamander Hill: may beauty be always before you and strength be in your wild, raw hearts. To my wonderful team at Weiser—Peter Turner, Judika Illes, Jane Hagaman, Mike Conlon, Kathryn Sky-Peck, Ashley Benning, Be Engler, Ellen Varitimos, my cheerleaders Bonni Hamilton, Eryn Eaton, and Michelle Spanedda—my deepest thanks.

Foreword

Iawake to the cool breeze of late September 2018 in Asheville, North Carolina. I grab a light cotton robe and shuffle into the kitchen for a morning cup of Hecate tea. The whistle of the tea kettle, the clink of the bottles on the refrigerator door—these sounds ground me in the moment of early morning, the sky still pink. I open the door to the little house and exit the screen door, settling into the chair on the porch to breathe in the morning dew. The little house is the main character of this story, each generation seemingly adding their own personality.

It's such a personal thing to be invited to be a guest in someone's home. You get to know them in a way that is impossible outside of such close quarters. I have known Byron nearly ten years, and she has always regarded me as a trusted friend and co-conspirator. She is forever exposing new depths and constantly evolving her practice and the minds of those around her.

The house belongs to one H. Byron Ballard. Although it seems funny to say that anyone can own such a treasure. Rather, Byron belongs to this house. I was in town for the week as a part of the book tour for *Blackthorn's Botanical Magic*, and Byron had offered me the use of her beautiful home. In reading Byron's own *Seasons of a Magical Life*, I picture the land that inspired the year-long journey you hold in your hands. It doesn't just explain the year; it drives us to cycle with the land on which you find yourself and, in doing so, reach who you are, with less hustle and bustle. You find the part of yourself that you cherish with your morning rituals, before society takes its pound of flesh.

As I'm writing, it is 2020, and it seems every month of this year teaches us to find new depths in ourselves, rather than the outside world; to build our communities, to tend the soil of our home and nurture the roots of family, no matter what that family looks like, chosen or built. This book is an antidote to fear, panic, hopelessness, and helplessness. It teaches us not just what the seasons are, but how we can reinvent the seasons in our lives, to work in concert with the land, rather than trying to bend the land to our will.

"We wander into this place of mist and soil, of flood, and of the desire for things we can barely name because the culture we have lived in has lost it, sold it, and buried it." This book is about reclaiming the soul of your land, as well as yourself. Projects for the entire year help you live, not just in the moment, but of the moment as well. The skills imparted by the author are things that threaten to leave us in a generation or two: building a fire, foraging, making your own furniture polish, brewing, dyeing, sewing, knitting, and soap-making. These are all skills that bring us out of our frustrations and allow the soul to shine through. Unearth your soul while you ground your feet and let yourself brighten to the seasonal tasks that can bring you comfort, peace, joy, and centering.

This year-long journey walks us through the resources we can utilize for the growth and establishment of the home, as well as projects that can be done with children or grandchildren. It is about building: A life. A home. A homestead. A community. Inside there are foraging tips to get to know the local flora and fauna, as well as fill your belly and introduce you to local medicinal herbs. Self-sufficiency is wonderful, but working together lessens the load for everyone.

When we write books like the work Byron has put together here, we think about our communities, but we can never imagine how far those communities extend. It's funny, I have written three books, and I'm always delighted and surprised when I meet someone from a distant place who has read them. One of my earliest fan letters was from Tibet. These treasures will outlive us, and untold lives will be touched. We can't foresee the impact, but knowing that it touched even one person brings life and meaning to this work. Thank you so much, Byron, for helping us to walk outside and journey within.

—Amy Blackthorn, high priestess and
author of *Blackthorn's Botanical Magic,*
Blackthorn's Botanical Brews, and *Sacred Smoke*

I am so in love with this place, these hills, this ragged wound of a world.
I am.

—the Author

Et dominabitur a mari usque ad mare,
et a flumine usque ad terminos terrae.
He shall have dominion also from sea to sea,
and from the river unto the ends of the earth.

—Psalm 72:8

Preface

The Gabbleratchet and the Deepening Dark

*My continued exploration of homeliness must also embrace this season of length-
ening dark. For those of you who are unfamiliar with this use of the word
homely, in this context it means "homelike, cozy, safe," as the British use the
term. (I tend to play with language—as you will soon discover—so unfamiliar or tweaked words and phrases will be found in the glossary at the end of the
book.) At the Goddess Temple this morning, the priestess led us in an exploration of this dark time and the importance of sitting in it, being in it, learning
from it. In the guided meditation, I saw the remaining days in this intense
agricultural year stretch before me like a long hallway—or better, one of those
collapsible spy-glasses, one that grows denser as it stretches towards the Solstice.*

In my spiritual tradition, we cheerfully refer to the months after the
Green (Summer) Solstice as the Time of the Long Dying, and particular attention is paid to the few weeks after Samhain, the final Harvest.
These are the weeks, the hours of the deepening dark, when messages
from the unseen people are lessening in frequency but more potent, more
desperate for a hearing.

Breathing into the meditation, with the dark spy-glass clattering ahead
into the shadowed future, a distant sound spun into my mind's ear. Dim,
closer, close—as in nature, they wing their way northward past my window. The Gabbleratchet passed through and over and around me. Wild
geese flying free, high above the black river of Samhaintide descending.

I am counting down the darkening days now, watching every sunset, one eye on the clock. Earlier, earlier—the rose fingers of cloud and expectation caress the western mountains, spotlighting the edge of the horizon and the silhouette of the silver birch tree. And the night rises up on all the other sides, flowing in to fill the void of the lost day.

This is our world now, in these last days of the old agricultural year. There is an invitation in this early exchange of light and shadow and in the long nights. Surely part of that invitation is for each of us to sleep more deeply, to rest more fully, to practice radical self-care as well as healing. But the other part of that invitation is the opportunity—and possibly the requirement—to sit with the shadow, and in the shadows, and to acknowledge our connection, our profound debt to these shadows.

This book is an invitation to modern Pagans to return to a simpler and quieter time, either literally or virtually, through letters from a small forest-farm in the southern highlands of the Appalachian Mountains. It looks at the agricultural year as a starting space for a deepening of Earth-centered spirituality. Borrowing a conceit from English writer Dorothy Hartley, the book begins with a set of back-stories to ease the reader into a place between the toil of the pre-Industrial Era and the uncertainty of the modern one, a place where the fast-moving stress of modern life can be affected by a better connection not only to the natural world but also to the elegant expression of the year as communicated through seasonal festivals and celebrations. The essays are set in the beginning, not only to give the reader a map of our journey but also to introduce some ideas that will better inform that journey. The back-stories form the legend of the map, as well as the compass rose. The chapters are broken into four seasons, with the Quarter Days a highlight within each, and include simple skills that accompany each marker in the year. The book wraps up with a chapter on spiritual and physical immersion into these seasons whether the reader finds herself on a farm in the country, in a condo in the city, or at any place in between.

If we are to step forward with more courage and less fear, if we are to feel empowered and also know the uses of that power—we must sit in this uncomfortable, feral, and dangerous darkness. We must come into relationship with the shadow and welcome the wisdom that resides in, permeates, and rules this endarkenment.

Do you see them now, as you peer into your own spy-glass? Can you hear their approach, flying southward, following the path of the old river? As the fierce cry of the Gabbleratchet explodes in our hearts, we are called to wing our own way into the dark, the shadow, the end that always—always!—signals the inevitable beginning.

Introduction

Notes from a Small Forest-Farm

It turned cold again in the night, and wet. Driving home through the lane closures and maddening traffic, I rest my eyes on the hills behind my cottage. It's warmer now, and the phenomenon that this region is known for begins its ascension from the forest floor. Wisps of cloud wiggle up the tree trunks, linger for a moment, then continue their journey to the sky. The Smoky Mountains are aptly named.

The way clears ahead of me, and there's not much road left between me and the little house. This part of town has little to commend it though it is within spitting distance of the opulent Biltmore House, center of George Vanderbilt's estate. That place is a tourist attraction now, with a winery, good restaurants, and expensive shops. Locals buy annual passes so they can walk the manicured grounds with their dog companions.

Car repair shops line the road I'm traveling, bordered by a paint store, a sub shop, and the inevitable craft brewery. The buildings are old but not in a valuable or attractive way. Still I like this place because it feels real, working-class. I wish there were an old-fashioned feed and seed store along this road, with chicks in the Spring and brassica starts for Fall planting. Those sorts of stores are rare now with big-box retailers selling plants and seeds, and mail-order houses that will ship chicks directly to your house.

The cycles we follow here—at the little house with its peculiar farm—are the same cycles our Ancestors learned when they left their nomadic lifestyle behind. They became farmers and growers, soil scientists and weather experts. The transitional generations must have been exciting and terrifying as they learned the ways of land and wind and water. Domesticating animals, saving seed for next year's crops, food processing and storage—all technologies we take for granted now—show necessity was the mother of all these inventions.

At last I turn onto the rutted and crooked driveway and pull the old Toyota all the way to the end, near the trinity of bird baths overlooking the raised beds. Birds are everywhere here, singing us awake in the morning, calling us to look out the back door to see what the farm's crow family is fussing about in the woods. No planter is safe from the songbirds' nesting, and I look forward to seeing their reaction to the small flock of chickens that will be joining the residents of the farm sometime next year.

The cottage is a small house but not a stylish "tiny house." It was built during the Second World War by a group of amateurs using materials available in wartime America. There is a front porch that runs the width of the house and a back porch half its size. Two years ago, my friend and handyman Arjuna painted it a warm sage green, and it is trimmed in terracotta.

Back of the house, as we say here in the mountains, is a forest of hardwoods—poplar, oak, and maple. Less than an acre, it boasts trails and scat from a variety of migratory visitors. The small folks are most often seen: groundhogs, field mice, rabbits, possums, and birds. But we have also been visited by bears, deer, and turkeys. Crows wake us in the morning and red-tailed hawks are unbothered by the workings of the smallholding below.

"Wake, work, wonder, and sleep" has become my mantra as I learn the ways of simple farming in a complex culture. My spirituality is stretched in this place and made somehow easy. Standing on the back porch and smelling the air, it is evident when Spring has arrived or when rain can be expected. Listening, the silence of Winter snow gives us an indication of how long the cold will last.

This little farm is a crucible for practical knowledge, but it is also a temple to the Divines I follow and, sometimes, listen to. The trees above, the medicinal plants below, and the insects and animals that call this place home are generous with wisdom about my practice as a farmer, a witch, and a Pagan.

I plan to share that wisdom within these pages with the hope that you, gentle reader, will get the sense of the importance of this primal connection and how dangerously close humankind is to losing its place in our threatened biosphere.

Where are the Pagans in all this? Many of us believe that the planet is holy ground: not just churches, synagogues, mosques, and Mount Sinai, but the whole shebang. The planet as the Greek deity Gaia is considered by some to be the living body of a living goddess. One would think it only natural that the rapidly growing global Pagan community would take leadership at this crucial time, that we would step forward to talk about our genuine and loving relationship to the land and the web of life. In a spirit of fellowship and community we might assist neighbors of other spiritual traditions to return to right relationship with the natural and sacred world. Where are the councils of elders, where the interfaith dialogue on these issues? Where are the Pagans?

Some Pagans are cleaning up streams, picking up litter, and sitting on interfaith councils, but in my experience their numbers are small. Some Pagans are working within their larger communities to create tribal units that answer to the old gods by preserving or recreating perceived old ways and following the cycles of the agricultural year. But the majority of Pagans, as far as I can tell, are sitting in front of computer screens, creating cyber-communities. We are posting our endless opinions in various chats, and we are doing what tribal folk love to do: we are fighting. We can't agree to be called *Pagan* because that's a Roman word used by Christians and it doesn't apply to all the myriad cultures that make up the Neo-Pagan movement, as it used to be called. Some of us prefer *Heathen* to *Pagan* and have the scholarship to back it up. Some people have tried the awkward phrase *Earth religionist* in an attempt to be as inclusive and comprehensible as possible. But some of the Reconstructionists and Traditionalists have sent up a hue and cry that their spirituality is not Earth-centered and never was and that nobody is going to get away with saying it is. Some of us don't like *Pagan* or *Heathen* because the words are too loaded with centuries of baggage. Half the culture doesn't know what *Pagan* means in the modern sense, and we must constantly explain ourselves and our motives.

This was brought home to me as I read a quote from the founder of a multifaith organization of which I was once an active part. He made a statement that ended with "teaching adherents to marginalize, paganize and plain old despise people of other beliefs." *Paganize?* What does that mean exactly in a multifaith peace organization that includes Pagans? Does it mean to make people into Pagans with a capital P? I hardly think so. It means to demonize, to alienate. So are Pagans demons or aliens? And why would a spiritually savvy interfaith leader feel he could use such a word without being castigated for it? Why indeed? Because words have multiple meanings and some of our work is about repeating our spiritual "elevator speech" over and over.

We say we are people of the land, we Pagans, and many of us follow an agricultural cycle that we call the Wheel of the Year. Using the cycles of this farming adventure as a springboard, I invite you to look deeply into what we practice and to find new—and renewed—meaning there.

Welcome.

Part One

Reaching Bedrock:
Background Essays

The way of life explored throughout this book did not spring up like chickweed—fully formed and ready to eat. It's the result of trial and error, of a somewhat consistent practice and a curious mind. The first part of this book winds its way through some of the ideas and discoveries that undergird the other sections. In it, the reader will find clues about how we as a species got where we are and ways to think about new engagement—acknowledged kinship—as well as an invitation to re-enchant the world. Come explore all that with me as we wander into the Wheel of the Year.

CHAPTER ONE

Animism, Mutual Aid, and Permaculture

Years back, I was working for a private prep school that attracts students from all over the world. Originally a boys' school, it now opens its doors to young women as well as commuter students. I was there to design sets and lighting for the drama program and to supervise a crew of students assigned to that department. My unusual spiritual bent inspired the chaplain to ask me to speak about Earth religions as part of a chapel program. He was later dismissed for his lack of foresight about that failure of judgment. I spoke in a beautifully appointed chapel to a mostly bored group of smart teenagers. Afterwards I stood at the doorway with the chaplain and shook hands with the students as they left the building. Three African students waited for me. They were confused by my talk and wanted a little more information about my belief system. After a brief dive into alternative verbiage, one of them smiled and nodded. "You are an animist," he proclaimed and the other two immediately understood. They left me, talking animatedly about the "animist teacher." I assume it was not their parents who called the headmaster to complain.

They were correct, of course. I am an animist, and I suspect most humans begin life understanding the idea that everything around them is alive and has a soul and personality. It's easy to see that with animals and birds, a little more difficult with trees and other plants. When we come

3

to consider rocks, lakes, and mountain ranges, the concept may be a little harder to ken.

Most people lose this animated world as they grow up, go to school, have a peer group. They are told that their earliest notions of personhood are flawed and most certainly "not real." We humans are animals that live in groups, and the opinion of the group has a profound influence on our way of thinking as well as our way of seeing.

Animism: How I Returned to an Acknowledged Kinship

The rear-end of the forest-farm lies at the base of a mountain so that in a drive south to attend to farm business, the bulk of the mountain rises higher the nearer one comes to its roots. There are antennae on the top—cell-phone towers and our public radio affiliate and who knows what else is up there. The road that brings you to the farm ends at the base of the mountain in an area of close woods. Signs proclaiming "No Trespassing" remind us that not all places welcome our wandering and may hold the secret knowledge that there is a winding pathway not only up the mountain but perhaps into it.

It is intriguing to think of a hollow mountain, and, if we consider it logically, the coal mines north and west of here *are* hollowed out mountains. When I travel to southern Ohio to spend time at Wisteria Nature Preserve, I drive up I-77, whose path leads deep into two mountains, the tunnels brightly lit. Not much romance or magic there. Except—if you drive that way often, you lose some of the fear of the manic drivers around you and can begin to reach out into the energy of the mountain.

Caves are an entryway into mountains. An overhang offers shelter, but a cave system with winding and sometimes treacherous burrows offers an explorer the sense of being in the belly of the hill, inside the womb of a living creature.

The idea of hollow hills is scattered throughout myth and legend. They serve as burial places and are therefore the province of the dead—both those at rest and those who walk about to interfere out-side the doorway to the living world. Hollow hills contain the things and beings that the self-styled civilized have left behind, willingly and know-ingly—the things that frighten us and intrigue us. These are the pieces of our collective human soul that had to be jettisoned to make us the lonely and angry creatures we've become, weighed down by all the layers of civ-ilization we have accrued.

Perhaps the best known is the Venusberg, an idea I return to again and again. The Venusberg is a mountain in European folklore that was popular from the lays of the Middle Ages all the way up to Richard Wagner's opera *Tannhäuser.* It is a familiar motif—a hollow mountain that holds treasures and beautiful people—and in the case of the Venusberg it also holds the goddess Venus. It is removed from the ordinary world and promises peace and a life lived without care or anxiety. These hollow hills appeal to me because I live in and come from old mountains and because in some of the legends, things and people that are no longer valued in the human realm choose to go into the mountain, with its heavenly reputa-tion, and to bide there for all time.

But another hollow mountain sneaks in through the story of the Pied Piper of Hamelin. The town is overrun with rats, and a Jack-like character dressed in jester's clothes appears before the town council. He has a plan to rid the town of the destructive and potentially plague-ridden crea-tures—he will use his magic flute (another interesting motif) to lure them into the river, where they will all be drowned. He names his price, and they eagerly agree—anything to get rid of the rats! Anything! The piper does his magic, and rats come from all their nesting places and follow his dancing steps down to the banks of the river. He continues to play as they scurry into the river to meet their demise. His task accomplished, he is praised by the people of the town as he walks back to the council to col-lect his fee. But that's where it all goes haywire because the rich burghers of the town are indeed relieved that the problem is solved but are not so quick with the payment. After all, they reckon, the rats are drowned and can't come back.

Much like the elected officials in our own day and time, they begin to find fault with the hired help and try to back out of their part of the deal. They are shocked to think he would still require so much gold for such a simple task, one that took so little effort. He waits patiently as the betrayal plays out. Suddenly the grateful people of the town are eyeing him with suspicion, and the burghers are laughing at his clothes. The mayor tosses him a few coins and tells him he's lucky to get that, since the mayor is starting to think that the stranger was responsible for the infestation to begin with. The stranger turns on his heel and leaves the council chamber, never to return. He sits on a rock pondering his revenge and their punishment, while the town congratulates itself on tricking the stranger and living rat-free.

The stranger returns the following Sunday, while all the adults are in church. He is dressed in hunter green now, and his tune is different. The children of the town come out from wherever they are, lured out by the sweetness of the flute. They follow the piper, not to the river, but up into the mountains, dancing merrily to the piper's tune. When they reach the foot of the mountain, the stranger gathers the children around him and tells them they are going to a place of magic and adventure, where the tables are laden with cakes and sweets and no one will spank them or make them work or go to bed hungry. With a wave of his hand, a doorway opens in the side of the mountain. He stands with one foot in the mountain and one in the meadow, and he plays another tune. The children laugh and run into the mountain, singing. When the last child has disappeared into the darkness, he bows his head to the outside world and turns to join them, as the doorway closes and the sound of the flute fades away. Only one child is left outside, a boy with a short leg who could not keep pace with the others. He cries to see the door close and returns to the village to let them know what has happened.

It is not only hollow hills that feature so prominently and vividly in our cultural imagination but also hills that stand alone, that rise from a plain or valley. Think for a moment of Kilimanjaro and Everest and Fuji. These are naturally occurring mountains that draw us, that cause us to dream of what those heights contain and how we could be transformed by the ordeal of traveling to the summit.

Other hills have been fabricated by hand by our Ancestors. The people who moved throughout the Southeast and Midwest of the United States before European contact were so proficient at building these extraordinary structures that we have come to refer to them and their culture—about which we know little—as the Mound Builders. Engineering wonders were left for us to explain, explore, and try to intuitively understand their purpose. The Serpent Mound is best viewed from the sky in order to get the total effect of this marvel. The mountain that drew me, that haunted me, lies in Wiltshire, in England, and is part of the Neolithic complex we call Avebury.

Silbury Hill

It loomed so large in my soul and in my head, like the Devils Tower–obsessed man in the film *Close Encounters of the Third Kind*. It was there in dreams, in waking visions, lingering in my peripheral sight. Flat-topped and squashed, it isn't like the old hills of home. Silbury Hill is human-created, the largest mound of its kind in Europe, and the latest theory is that it came about by accident, the chalk-and-stone slag heap of the bank-and-ditch monument that we call Avebury.

But every time I thought of the hill, Peter Gabriel's song "Solsbury Hill" got stuck in my head. The names are so similar that I had always assumed that "Solsbury" was a corruption of Silbury. Both are typical of the odd and generally human-made hills that seem to dot the landscape of Britain and much of western Europe. But the two hills are different. Solsbury is a low and natural hill that once had a hillfort on top and was occupied for a good long time. This is hardly an unusual thing in Britain, where it seems most villages have remnants of a hillfort or a couple of lonely standing stones within their boundaries. Silbury is a feat of human engineering that has been excavated a couple of times, and not much has been found on either occasion. One hill endured human occupation for many generations; the other hill was merely the detritus of a great and ancient building project.

One of my research trips to Britain afforded me the opportunity to visit Avebury after an absence of many years, after my obsession with the hill was firmly implanted. Most of the time it made no sense to go there—it was out of the way. This trip took me from Cornwall to Yorkshire, though, and it didn't seem an impossible thing at all.

There isn't a train to Avebury, so I took the train as far as I could and then got a bus—a "coach," in Brit-speak—to Avebury, where I'd reserved a B&B. Finding the B&B was an adventure in and of itself, with piskies, church lych-gates, and muddy fields. The landlady regaled me with stories of ley lines and crop circles, and I slept badly that night, dreams of flat-topped hills haunting the darkness.

The weather the next day was perfect, not too hot, the sky bright with fat clouds. I guided my way by siting the church steeple and zigzagging along until I came to the dirt path into the village. The modern village is situated within the stone circle and there is a very nice pub with decent food as well as a place called the Henge Shop, which features postcards, souvenirs, silver jewelry, books, and a cooler with Cornettos.

It felt as if there were a magnet buried in my chest and it pulled me forward, calling to its opposite somewhere in the heart of the hill. I walked slowly; the shades of all those who had come this way before seemed clustered at my elbows, me leading the procession down the processional way.

A song came into my head as I reached the High Street. It was, of course, Peter Gabriel's "Solsbury Hill." I didn't remember many of the words but did recall the melody. These shreds of lines couldn't connect into a verse, but there were enough bits to keep me humming as I studied the directional signs that led me past the pub and onto the path through the close-enough-to-touch stones of the henge and out onto the sloping West Kennet Avenue—The Avenue.

The path took me past a grove of oaks, situated on a steep hill to my left. A single crow called to me, distracting me from me, tempting me. Rocks made a stairway into the grove, and I put my foot on the bottom one, then stopped. Silbury Hill was less than a mile away, waiting. But the leathery green of the leaves with the blue of the sky showing through their pattern dazzled me. I stood there listening to their little voices, waiting. The crow was joined by a friend, and they chatted above me, turning their beaks to the side to watch me as they talked. I stepped up onto the first step, then the second, and in that way, crows now silently observing me, I came to stand amidst those trees, on that little hill.

I looked in the direction of Silbury, and the crows restarted their conversation, joined now by two others. They hardly glanced my way, as though their intention had been to bring me to this odd place with its trees neither old nor young, but leafing out nicely on this fine April day. I sat down on a rock and leaned against the trunk behind me, humming Gabriel's tune as best I could remember. One crow hopped down then, a few feet from where I sat, turning her large head to watch me. My humming grew louder, and the crow made a chirruping noise in her throat.

The tune was stuck in my head, and I softly sang the few lines I remembered. The crow stepped away then and looked back over her shoulder, dismissing me. I turned my ear to the tree trunk and listened. The sap of the tree made a song in my head that replaced "Solsbury Hill" for a time. I couldn't identify the tune; it wasn't one I knew. But it had drums in it and a tin whistle and a sound like a jaw-harp. It was faint but discernible, like a radio turned down low.

The crows were away, and it was time for me to do likewise. I kissed the tree's bark and made my way down the stones and back on the path to the hill.

It is an unconsciously regal walk, and I made it in the center of the Avenue with its ragged border stones. My step was deliberate but not slow. After all, I had been waiting over a year for this meeting, this revelation. I headed to the way-finding signs and over the stile, onto the hill from which I could see *the* hill. It wasn't a hard climb through this cow pasture, but it was an ascent and I found myself slowing my pace. I passed a large bush, filled with traditional prayer strips called clouties, and knew I'd spend time there on the way back.

There it was, close but untouchable. I could have been at its foot but intuitively felt that the distance and the image of the entire hill were important. A cow grazed close by and looked up as I dropped my backpack. There it was ahead of me on this clear day. Squatting, waiting.

There was a possibility that I'd feel disappointed, that this adventure would end in an anticlimax. But there it was.

I watched it as one would watch a distant mystery, as though a door might open in the side of the hill. Grounding myself, I waited—waited to see what I would do or feel or know. There was a wind chime amongst the clouties on the bush below me, and it sounded now, though there was no breeze that I could notice. The cow raised her head and first looked at me then turned to face the hill, a sight she must have seen every day. Raising my hand, I traced the paths across its face with my forefinger, wondering if I looked like a modern Merlin spinning magic with gesture and will.

A bird I didn't know sang on the fence. I watched the hill.

It was then I got the distinct feeling that the hill was also watching us, watching me. Casually, glancing over to a scene that played out every day. A human, some cows, birds singing, cars and lorries on the A4. Always the same, always different. Observing with minimal curiosity, the way cats do when they first wake from the sunny windowsill that is their bed.

I sat down, hard, at the edge of the pasture, near the fence. The hill knew me, though it had no reason to do so. Or maybe it knew my type and lumped me in with the other humans who came in search of meaning, of magic. It knew me and there was neither curiosity nor fear, merely an acknowledgment that we were occupying the same basic space.

The hill beneath my legs and bottom was warm, and I fancied it shifted minutely, a nod to its odd sister. The cow dropped her head then and slowly grazed away from me. The bird took flight, its airy path taking it back towards the pub and the chance of cold chips and bits of bread.

Only I remained on that communicating hill, waiting, grateful for a gift I couldn't name: a knowing of the kinship that bound us to each other—bird, hill, cow, woman. The Peter Gabriel tune came back into my ear, and I sang the few lines I remembered as I rose.

The cloutie tree held the prayers and hopes of so many people, and I left a silver ring (taken from the collection on my left thumb) in thanks. The cow followed me halfway down the path then turned away towards home. I don't know how long we stood there while I slowly garnered what was being shown me. But the Sun was moving in its seemingly downward path, and it was time to go.

I come from a place of hills, of old mountains and old magic. Wandering the cow paths on the mountain of my childhood gave me the leisure to observe, the sense to avoid what should be avoided, and the quiet in which to imagine that I was merely part of the landscape there. I felt as sturdy as the ridgeline and as tall as the tallest old locust tree, but I was free to go home and eat a bologna sandwich and sleep in my own narrow bed. It was only when I left that world and tried to find myself amongst bigger buildings and people who didn't think or act like me that I discovered not everyone felt that way. For some people, this familial feeling I had for soil and clouds and garter snakes was peculiar and possibly dangerous. Their religions and their cultures told them that the land—the world itself—was dangerous and filthy, something to be avoided if one were to remain healthy and connected to the Divine. They could not have been farther from the truth, but I had no idea how to argue the point with them and so I let them go. But I continued to wonder—how can humans believe they are not connected to the biosphere, are only lodgers here, and are happily serial abusers of the world they despise?

Eden, or Why We Left the Garden

Before we were kicked out, ashamed of our animal nakedness, we were given orders to name every critter in the garden, and once the magic ritual of naming was complete, the garden and everything in it was ours to do with as we thought fit. Free fruit and veg, happy animal friends, and prime real estate. Too bad about that snake thing. Too bad we couldn't obey a set of fairly simple rules.

Along with our strategically placed fig leaves, we left the garden with one thing—the certainty that we were special in the eyes of the Creator and that, even though the garden was no longer our home, we were the boss in the great world beyond the sword-wielding angels. We were given dominion, by God, and we meant to dominate.

And since we are more special than—and therefore superior to—elk or newts or sponges (not to mention minerals, petroleum, and trees), it was up to us to tame and control nature, to cut civilization from the heart of the wilderness. We gave up the religious observances that tied the course of our lives to the agricultural year and took to ourselves spiritual systems that further alienated us from the natural and possibly dirty, sin-filled, and soul-endangering world. We set our eyes on a heavenly kingdom and simply endured the horrors of living life on a planet that supplied our every want and need. As civilization progressed, we moved farther and farther from the gods of our tribal Ancestors and from our connection to the natural world. Sacred groves were chopped down and white spires pointed our way out of this cesspool of sin and towards our real home and our heavenly Father. Rural lives were exchanged for urban ones, and the Industrial Age brought us everything our hearts desired—for a price. The powerful cultural entity called the Church turned its attention to saving the souls and bodies of the poor, left dispossessed by Western success.

But now, in the twenty-first century, as environmental degradation comes to a place where it cannot be dismissed or denied, the more liberal and even moderate Christians are embracing the notion of "stewardship of God's creation." Christian authors have begun to concern themselves not only with justice and civil rights issues but also the ecological disarray confronting the citizens of planet Earth.

Listening for the Hoofbeat of God

Working in an indie bookstore for fifteen years, I sometimes would walk quickly past a new book and misread the title. That happened with a pretty book on Celtic Spirituality—a Pagan-flavored Christianity that was all the rage in the 1990s—called *Listening for the Heartbeat of God* by poet John Philip Newell. I saw it as "Listening for the Hoofbeat of God," and it set me thinking about how we encounter the living spirit of nature as an anthropomorphized being. Time now for us to look past the Green Man figures in European art and the deities like Pan—which are a helpful entry point for many Pagans—to an intuitive knowing (kenning) about the webs of being and how they both connect and renew.

We are not separate from these other gods, these wild gods, these green gods unless we choose exile from them. We can allow the green of the world to seduce us, luring us into its herbal clutches. We can stretch ourselves out in a field of red clover and feel the spirit of soil and rain rise up to meet our seeking, thirsty soul. We can select a few herbs native to the land with which we dwell and learn everything we can about them and whisper their names, chanting our way to herbal bliss. As we learn about them, one by one, we form an alliance with them. Then we move to another one and then another until we can stand at the edge of a gravel parking lot edged with them and recite their names like a lover, like wild poetry. This love story can lead to making salve from their leaves and saving the small spike of seeds for that day when we will live in the country, with friends and pastures and fields. But today, here, in this less-than-primal setting, we can touch the mystery.

Animism as a Political and Economic Force

There are still some places in the world where the country folk will talk about how a certain area is peopled by ghosts or little people, but the larger culture has mostly lost the notion of a place having a soul. With the reemergence of Earth religions and spiritual philosophies, however, we are seeing the intentional re-sacralizing of the landscape.

We don't talk at any length about the spiritual dimensions of our communities, unless we are talking about specifically spiritual communities or are our faith representative in a multifaith discussion group. In more tribal times, all of Earth was spirited, peopled with spirits indigenous to a land base or to a spring or an outcropping of stone. That spiritual energy seems confined now to "places of worship" and "the Holy Land," which may be one of the results of the monotheists that conquered most of the known world. They strove to contain the powers of the unseen inside designated structures—we are fortunate indeed that those powers can't be managed or contained for long.

So much of the interconnected global economy is dominated by capitalism and the language found in Genesis that is foundational to these worldwide movements towards "civilization" and the domestication of sacred space, which include privatizing social welfare programs (including health care) and enclosing common lands. We are still trapped by that language and the philosophies that have sprung from it, whether consciously or not. As we explore and deepen our acknowledged kinship with All That Is, one of the systems we would be wise to consider is the economic one under which we live and that moves hand in hand with the ways in which we organize ourselves—our political systems. When we incorporate the ancient notion of animism into our understanding of how we govern ourselves, how we are governed by those we select to govern us, and how we trade within our local groups, we can begin to move from a philosophical notion into a way of living with each other on a planet that is treated with respect and, potentially, affection.

Transforming cultures from the inside out is slow work, but it may be the only way to achieve these long-term goals. As we watch the shuddering collapse of so many global systems, it is imperative that we return to the place we abide and study it carefully. While it is certainly invigorating and dramatic to shake up the power dynamics on a state or national level, much of that work is not sustainable in any real sense. By embracing the cyclical change in the natural world, we can create as well as rediscover systems that serve the needs of people and planet. By re-localizing food, for instance, we can monitor those areas in our immediate region that have become food deserts, either through unconscious overdevelopment or racism or classism. Resources can then be brought to bear on reversing the tide of poor resource management. To do so on a national or even global level has become too daunting a task to undertake.

So we will take it a bite at a time.

We will begin with economics—something few, if any, really understand. At its simplest, these are systems by which society earns or accumulates the goods for survival. Self-sufficiency was a matter of pride in the Appalachia where I grew up, and because of that people worked very hard to take care of themselves and kept an eye on the extended families that are a hallmark of the culture, as well as on those who had fewer skills for self-reliance. Money was needed to do two things—pay taxes and purchase the things that could not be grown, hunted, or made. But this made for an exhausting and short life, with few luxuries.

Fast-forward to now, when most people have jobs outside the home for which they are paid a wage and with this wage they are expected to purchase all the things their Ancestors grew or made. In some cases they are working as hard as those farmers, and they certainly have more amenities—electricity, indoor water and plumbing, Internet service—as well as luxuries—dishwashers, multiple cars, more clothes than can possibly be worn out. But the satisfaction is often outweighed by the anxiety over job security and rising prices.

Some of the earliest known writings are accountings of goods and services. When we moved from hunter-gatherer societies, which are generally believed to have shared the bounty of both hunting and gathering with the whole of the tribal unit, into farming and herding communities, tallying amounts available for immediate consumption or held in store for leaner times became important. What we are looking at is the first piece of economics—the use of natural resources. Most economic systems are based on a maximizing of available natural resources to sustain and enhance human life and to gain something through the exchange of goods and services.

However, in a system in which the natural world has intrinsic value—not because of products that humans consume, but because it is a living being made up of interwoven webs of being—our choices will by necessity change.

Political Systems

Humans have always had trouble with governance. Our written history is consumed with our quest to govern our families, our villages, our nation-states, but especially ourselves, our wants and desires. Whole religions obsess over control and governance. People generally like to think for themselves and do what feels best for them and their immediate circle of influence and affection. That means that if we are to work successfully in societies, we may have to compromise some of our personal desires in order for the society as a whole to function and be successful.

Politics is the mechanics we use to sustain governance. It is based on putting in place and keeping in place a group or individual who either leverages a great deal of authority and power or who has the largest base of support for their ideas. Political decisions are made depending on which of those concepts is uppermost for the society at a particular time.

I used the word *successful* and want to return to that briefly. Cultures—and the societies that make them up—collectively determine the definition of successful. For many, it is meeting all the needs and most of the wants of the people who make up that society. For some it is more important to be seen as having an excess of those things—of being "rich"—and when a culture has excess, there may be a perceived need to protect those goods and services from other "less successful" groups. This may require a means of defense—an army or other policing entity. This group's function is only to protect those goods and services from forces outside the society that may seek to take them away. So a society's success is measured by societal expectations around perceived status when compared to other societies.

It is interesting to note how these two things—economics and politics—can move hand in hand, one influencing the other and both having a profound effect on society. Now we come back to this idea of animism and how that weaves itself around and through these other ideas.

If we define animism as the idea that every thing and every being in the biosphere is ensouled, how might that affect the decisions we make about governance and economics? Our decision processes must change when we are no longer taking what natural resources we need from a dead planet, a place that has been given to us by a divine being for our use, over which we have been asked to be stewards. Our care for and consideration of others of our own species must necessarily change when we can finally perceive the webs of living that flow into and out of all of us, regardless of culture or creed.

Mutual Aid

As we draw in our spirals of influence and continue the process of re-localizing everything within those spirals, we come to see the larger culture as one of separation—some of it intentional, some of it imposed. There are nostalgic dreams of days "gone by" when neighbors helped each other out and families were in close proximity. Everyone was seemingly jolly and helpful, even in dire circumstances. This is ridiculous, of course. Throughout our long and twisted history, there have been people who are generally helpful and others who are helpful in a crisis, and then there have been those who are not only not helpful but are actually a hindrance. Every culture throughout the world and throughout our history—no matter how benevolently they share their story—has had people who were both, were all.

We can be influenced to lean one way or the other through the stories we tell. If it is the standard in your extended family, your neighborhood, or your town to be concerned for the welfare of others, you are more likely to follow suit. If you live in a place that is notorious for its parsimony and ruthless individualism, you may lean that way, regardless of your personal inclination. But even in cultures that favor one response over the other, there will be outliers who follow their own inclination in the face of what may be expected of them.

Minority and immigrant communities learn early on that helping their neighbor benefits themselves and boosts the survival rate of the group under the aegis of the dominant and dominating culture, whatever that may be. They learn to support each other's businesses, to take the extra steps necessary to keep the peace, and to render aid how and where they can. Poor neighborhoods have been especially good at sharing what few material goods they have.

It is a truism that rural families could always throw another couple of potatoes in the stew and bake more biscuits if a neighbor were going hungry, but that is the case in most communities. Children and elders especially can benefit from the generosity of their watchful neighbors in a culture that values mutual aid.

Although this term has become a buzzword in the last few years, mutual aid has been around for a very long time. It is defined as a system by which a particular set tends to the needs of the group and each member operates voluntarily, though sometimes under the direction of a small committee that keeps its fingers on the web of the group, often knowing what is needed before it has been expressed. The more you work for and with the group, the more status is achieved, though status is never the goal.

My neighborhood is rapidly gentrifying, and one of things I miss from years back is the community fundraisers that were the equivalent of a crowdsourcing fundraising site of the sort popular on social media outlets. The most popular event was the fish fry where you could, for a minimal amount—usually five dollars—get a disposable plate of fried fish, some cole slaw, and French fries. The cooking would have been going on all of the afternoon, and you might have had to take it home and reheat it. There would be signs all over the neighborhood about the recipient: someone needed help with medical bills or rent or getting a kid to summer camp. It was a chance to socialize a little, do some good, and not have to cook supper. At the end of the day, the money—no matter how much or how little—was presented to the recipient, who knew that their neighbors cared enough about their predicament that they had done this amazing thing.

I am writing about this in the past tense because it doesn't happen in my neighborhood anymore. But it is a thriving practice in lots of other places in my town and probably in yours.

The sharing of physical labor is another part of the idea of mutual aid. Whether through illness, injury, or age, some people especially in the suburbs may have trouble doing chores that used to be a normal part of their week. Cleaning gutters, mowing the lawn, even fetching the mail from the box at the end of the walk may become burdensome. In a setting of mutual aid, it is easy enough to coordinate with that neighbor and mow that yard when you mow your own, to bring the mail to the porch when you walk your dog, to put together a team of friends with a good ladder to take on the gutters in your elderly neighbors' houses on a fine Saturday afternoon. It then becomes an act of kindness bestowed by a group of friends, and the giving of this gift enriches giver as well as recipient.

Dorothy Day expressed this in much of her writing, and her concept comes from a place of expressed Christian charity. There is often the understanding in mutual aid societies that the work is predicated on the needs of the group and sometimes those needs are spiritual as well as physical ones. In the worlds we are envisioning, there is little difference between the physical and the spiritual, each tightly woven to the other. So to bake bread together to bring to the homeless camps or the support services for them is an act that can be filtered through our spiritual lens as Earth-abiding people.

Mutual aid is about taking responsibility for your community in whatever way your gifts allow. The broader the connection, the more likely it is that there will be someone who knows how to do anything the group needs.

There are some vibrant examples of how this can work. Many cities now have tool libraries—places where communally acquired tools are loaned out for a few days and then returned to the place that houses them. These are set up in a number of ways—some are nonprofit organizations run by volunteers who have gotten grants from seed companies or local growers to buy basic gardening and farming tools. These are checked out—sometimes with a deposit left until the tools are returned, especially with more valuable tools—and used for the project at hand. Some tool libraries are community-based, and one family has the stash in a shed in the back yard. This works best in established neighborhoods where people can hold each other accountable, where there is a generally high level of trust.

Another sort of library that is gaining in popularity is a seed library. These are sometimes held in actual community libraries where local growers who have saved or purchased more seed than they can use mark small envelopes with the kind of seed, fill and seal the envelopes, and tuck them into a box where seeds are arranged by alphabetical order.

In mutual aid societies, the people in the circle often know each other, and that leads to a strengthening of the kinship amongst their numbers. But some may choose, for whatever reasons, to remain anonymous in their giving. There are two interesting phenomena that have emerged in recent years that give people a way to share—to give—indirectly.

Little libraries first sprang up in more affluent suburbs and were ways people could trade books or get rid of books they had already read or no longer wanted. In the early days it was mostly books of the recent bestseller variety, and they were housed in water-tight, decorated boxes set on posts, like the ones that hold mailboxes. The door was held closed by a toggle or magnetic latch, and anyone could browse the shelf and take what looked interesting or leave a couple of books the homeowner might like.

Then those boxes started showing up in other kinds of neighborhoods, in urban community centers and in public housing, at middle schools and church parking lots. People left magazines, candy papers, and condoms as well, but the idea took root and the most stubborn of the little libraries keep on keeping on.

I first became aware of "blessing boxes"—small food pantries—through a group in South Carolina called Lowcountry Blessing Boxes. The concept is the same as the little libraries, but these are stocked with non-perishable food items, socks, personal hygiene items like toothbrushes, and Winter accessories like hats, scarves, and gloves in cold weather. These are often in specially built boxes—larger versions of the little libraries. But some are adapting newspaper boxes of the kind that hold daily papers for distribution for their blessing boxes. Placement for these boxes is key to reaching the demographic of people who actually benefit from them.

Those of us who choose to feed birds, Ancestors, and land spirits have the opportunity with these simple outreach ideas to extend this "feeding" to the people in our webs of life we don't know. The blessing boxes are almost always near an urban church, and the members take it upon themselves to check the box and refill as necessary. As animists, we may also choose to create these centers of hospitality or to partner with a church community that upholds our earthy values and do some of our spiritual work through these plain acts of giving—giving not to people we know or to whom we have familial obligations but to those with whom our obligations are societal and merely human.

When we fold the concepts of mutual aid into our conscious knowledge of the kinship of all the webs of being, we begin to understand how vast these webs are and how powerful a single tug of the silk can be.

Permaculture

Permaculture works hand in hand with animism though many people choose to practice one without the other. Animism feeds our longing for the primal connection, and permaculture makes that connection manifest through a series of design principles that tie the webs of being to the creation of manmade ecosystems based on observation of similar ecosystems found in nature. It is using those webs as a guide, as instruction for how we proceed in our own lives to strengthen and heal the cultures that birthed us.

These concepts draw heavily on resilience as a desired outcome of the designs and encourages acts of physical and spiritual rewilding to remove some of our imprinted history of colonization. Other components of permaculture include the idea of regenerative agriculture, which is one of the most healing parts of these processes.

These ideas of working with the natural world instead of against it were first codified by a couple of men, David Holmgren and Bill Mollison, both from Tasmania and both influenced by the natural farming methods that were being explored in various parts of the world. The techniques of no tilling, no herbicides or insecticides, and working to restore the ravages of industrial farming through regenerative agriculture were all part of this new concept of feeding humans without destroying the land that sustains us, spiritually as well as physically. To be separated from it, to willingly pull up and slice our roots, has been the destruction of us as a species. The only thing that will save us is this return to reconnection—to reroot ourselves in this perfect and tortured place.

I smile at the idea of permanence. Like you, I know that little is permanent in life and this is often very good thing. I embrace what permaculture means, however, because it is about *resilience* in the face of impermanence. There are solid online courses, books, and in-person intensives that will teach you the foundations of permaculture, and some will even give a certificate. But living with the land and not just on the land will give you many needed insights on how you should proceed.

I live in one of Asheville's oldest neighborhoods, where property values have soared in recent years. People congratulate us on our "investment," but what do higher property values do for people who have a commitment to a neighborhood and don't plan to sell in order to turn a quick profit? They raise property taxes, that's what, and open the floodgates for speculative land acquisition and rapid development.

But there should be in-fill housing in neighborhoods like mine where urban renewal took such a heavy toll, displacing longtime residents with the creation of the through-town expressway. Better another clapboard house slapped up between other little houses in a mill village than the foolish steep-slope development that has become so popular and so prominent in our area.

As these vacant lots are filled in, the character of neighborhoods changes, sometimes for the better, sometimes not. My old neighborhood used to have little grocery stores, churches, businesses along the river. Most houses had a little garden plot where vegetables were grown to add to the cook pot or to can for Winter. Many neighbors kept a few chickens for eggs and meat. There was a line in the backyard for drying clothes. It was an unremarkable blend of rural and urban living that could be found in most small towns in America. You could fish in the river, spend the morning cutting kindling, then catch the streetcar and go uptown for a movie. Because I grew up with stories of this place, I am nursing a special dream: I dream of a radical change in the lives of city-dwellers, one that I see creeping in on the edges of some neighborhoods. I dream of the ruralization of urban areas, backyards with gardens, chickens, goats for milking, sheep for wool.

To embrace these ideas of animism and permaculture—and their outgrowth in mutual aid—is to encounter what we have done to the land and then to go to the primal wounding of the species—which is what we have done to each other and to ourselves. To face our written history of willful destruction is to carry a burden too great for any one of us to bear alone without breaking entirely. This means we must approach this—the greatest work we have attempted as a species, the healing of the land as well as ourselves—knowing that we can be successful only when we link hands across cultures, when we reach backwards to our Ancestors and across the Borderlands to the Fair and Shining Ones. Our pride will be sacrificed, our honor restored, and the land—throughout the twisting pathways of Time—renewed. We will embrace and inhabit our former wilding as well as the kinship we have given away, or had taken away, or lost in the disregard and disrespect of our great Mother.

CHAPTER TWO

Tower Time and the Conceit of the Ever-Turning Wheel

I have written and taught extensively about the concept of "Tower Time," a phrase I coined over a decade ago to describe the uncertainty and rapid change of the era in which we live. In brief, Tower Time takes its name from the Tower card in the tarot deck. We are living in the time when the destructive top-down systems of patriarchy are collapsing under their weight of history, destruction, and misery. We see it in every hierarchical structure—medicine, government, education, religion. As these towers fail, there is a grasping at restructure and recalibration before they continue their inevitable descent. It is incumbent on humankind to reform our cultures in ways that are resilient, equitable, healthy, and thereby sustainable—a process I describe as circles on the ground. (For more on this see my book *Earth Works: Ceremonies in Tower Time*, Smith Bridge Press, 2018.)

When considering how time moves through the agricultural year, there's also another widely held conceit to examine. I refer to it as the "Ancient Calendar," though it may not be as ancient as we've been told. We understand that several western European cultures divided the year into only two seasons—Summer and Winter. These seasons meet at two pivotal points, and for that reason I have come to call them the Great Hinges of the year. For our purposes, Beltane to Samhain is Summer; Samhain to Beltane is Winter.

Many potential events and celebrations fall within each of these larger seasons, as do lunar celebrations of the Full, Dark and New Moon. The season of Summer includes four of the eight sabbats: Beltane, Midsummer, First Harvest, and Autumnal Equinox. Likewise Winter contains Samhain, Midwinter and the cultural New Year, Imbolc, and Vernal Equinox.

The eight-part ritual calendar is not ancient but may be based on ancient folk practices from pre-Christian and early Christian Europe. It has become a standard in modern Pagan practice, even as it generates controversy for its faux history. This Wheel of the Year conceit has a lot going for it though, as metaphor and as crucible.

Progress is measured in a particular way when time is linear. Culture, human life, and even history are seen to move forward, inevitably, into a future time, leaving behind the dead and the lost. The future is always new, always filled with possibilities. The past is dead and buried in the march forward. It feels efficient, like the top-down hierarchical systems that plague us today and have plagued us throughout human history. Humanity keeps moving forward, getting better, leaving our primitive origins in the past.

Those older systems that revolve around the human experience begin with personal practices, then move to the immediate family, and from there expand to the village, rippling outward only to begin again in the center. The agricultural year as we hold it comes down to birth, growth, reproduction, decline, death, repeat.

The Wheel is not dependent on myth or belief or story. It is divided neatly into two solstices and two equinoxes—solar events that are easily reckoned and observed. Regardless of hemisphere, there is a Winter Solstice and a Summer Solstice, a Vernal and an Autumnal Equinox. They require no deities, and yet they are filled with such wonder, such majesty.

These are the Quarter Days. They have marked our passage as humans for as long as we have noticed and responded to them. Since they are solar markers, we'll look at them through the lens of greater and lesser light.

The Winter Solstice marks the moment when the lengthening night within the time marker we call the day ends its increase and the time when the light portion of the day begins to increase. In the Northern Hemisphere it is the birth of the agricultural year. In the Southern Hemisphere, it marks the descent into more darkness, of rest, of gestation.

The Summer Solstice in the Northern Hemisphere marks the decline of the agricultural year, when harvests come to fruition and food is laid by for the coming months as the year winds down to the rest and quiet with lengthening nights. In the Southern Hemisphere, this solstice is, of course, the opposite.

The equinoxes are the mid-point in the hours of light and of dark, when they are of equal length. Every year, we experience the breath-holding moment when the night begins to lengthen to the fullness of the solstice. And on the opposite side of the Wheel, we honor the night when the dawning brings the promise of longer daylight and declining darkness.

These seasons, however they are expressed in the land where we live, move in a relentless cycle. For our purposes and those of the little forest-farm, we will refer to it as the agricultural year.

Between these Quarter Days, humans have developed a tidy crucible in which to either literally or metaphorically recreate the processes that lead to a sustaining and nurturing harvest. These are the Cross-Quarter Days, and there is some evidence that their genesis was in the fire festivals of the Celtic tribes of Europe. They are placed midway between the Quarter Days and generally celebrated at sundown the day before February I, May I, August I, and November I.

The Cross-Quarter Days are identified in several ways, but we'll use the ones most often employed. February is Imbolc, Christianized to Candlemas, the time when the Blessed Virgin was released from her segregation following childbirth. Imbolc is the earliest moment of Spring when the first greenlings appear in many places. It is sacred to the Gaelic goddess and later saint Brigid.

May is Beltane, which came down to the modern era as May Day. It is a fertility festival and later, a workers' holiday. So much of the folklore around this celebration has stayed with the culture—maypole, May baskets, May wine, and the Queen of the May.

August 1 is Lammas (the "loaf-mass" of the Saxons) or Lughnasadh (from the Irish). It is generally celebrated as the first of three harvest festivals, harvest being of prime importance. This is the grain harvest, hence "loaf mass."

Samhain—also the Christian festival of all saints and souls—marks the end of our year and is the final harvest, the beginning of Winter, and honored by some as the new year. It has manifested in the United States as a curious amalgam of Samhain and All Souls' Night that is called Hallowe'en. The eve before "all Hallows."

What the Cross-Quarters also provide is a time to plant (Imbolc), a time to tend (Beltane), a time to harvest and preserve (Lughnasadh), and a time to rest (Samhain). Whether we use these times to plant sweet peas and onions or to consider what we choose to manifest in our lives in the year to come, Imbolc fits the bill. We can dance around a maypole, put in potato eyes, tomato plants, and more green beans, or focus our good attention to our plans for the year and move them along, strategizing the next steps. The heat of Summer ripens the wheat, fattens the corn, yields generous quantities of squash to fill our tables, our freezers, and rows of pristine canning jars. It is also the time to claim what you've been growing in your life and reap the benefits of your months of attention and care. Though modern culture doesn't allow for it in any real way, Samhain (literally "summer's end") is the time when the land lies fallow, given space to rest from the intense labor of growing and making seed for the next year. And it is when humans would be wise to rest a little more as well, sleep a little more and be grateful for the fullness of their harvest, whether it is apples and eggplant or a book or advancement in your career.

The Quarter Days that came down to us through the Christian liturgical calendar are slightly different from the astronomical solstices and equinoxes or the ones on the standard Wheel of the Year. Lady Day falls near the Spring Equinox. Midsummer is the Summer Solstice. The Autumnal Equinox is honored with Michaelmas, though that date falls a week afterwards. And the feast of Christmas postdates the Winter Solstice by a few days.

Folklorically these Quarter Days offer some beautiful traditions that interface well with the Pagan cycle of celebrations, so we've folded them in where we can. In the case of a few of them, though, we've rethought them a bit and simply added them to the calendar.

Most of us are content to celebrate the holy days as they have come down to us in modern Paganism and may be loath to add anything else to a cycle of celebration that produces a holy day every six weeks. I worked for many years in an independent bookshop that was owned and frequented by Episcopalians. This gave me many opportunities to discuss theology, church history, and the work of the clergy in some depth with educated people who were interested in new ideas and interfacing ancient liturgy with social justice. They introduced me to the New Zealand Book of Common Prayer, which has some powerfully nature-based descriptions of the Christian Divines, as well as two clusters of days whose names were intriguing: Rogation Days and Ember Days. The names were evocative of an agrarian past, one connected to the land and to the fruits of human work upon and with it. As I explored these special days in the Christian calendar—days that seem to belong to the older denominations and less observed now than they were in generations past—I wondered whether they might be reclaimed and repurposed for my vision of the rewoven Wheel of the Year. We will begin with the Ember Days.

Ember Days and Embertide

With each Quarter Day comes an Embertide, which we will repurpose as a time to intentionally recharge our energies as well as our spiritual practice. The Christian calendar set aside three days in each season for fasting, abstinence, and prayer, but we have some other ideas.

The first week in March was aligned with planting. The second week in June was the time to pray for a bountiful harvest. The third week in September was the time to pray for a good year for grapes and the wine they produce. The second week in December was for keeping safe the seed for next year's planting.

The Church, both Catholic and Anglican, observes these four periods of three-day celebrations spaced out at regular intervals throughout the liturgical year. Each three-day celebration is called an *Embertide or Ember Days.**

There are folkloric roots, though, and these are the ones we are going to focus on for our earthy purposes. Since these days were originally used by the Church to deepen the spirituality of the communion of saints, we will appropriate that sentiment. Though the roots are unclear, they may have been based on earlier Roman agricultural festivals. Since the Romans are well known for stealing all their good ideas from elsewhere, we may surmise that the festivals were even older than Rome.

Four times a year, like the four cardinal directions: four times set aside to review where we are in our own spiritual work. These days can be used for assessing our regular practice or adding a regular or daily practice if we haven't been doing that. As in ancient times, we may do special rituals connected with the meaning of each triad. Offerings, in whatever way your tradition shares those, can be a focal point. These days can be used as a pause in the rolling year—days in which we especially honor our spiritual natures and gain new insights as to whether what we believe is reflected in what we do day by day.

---

* *https://angeluspress.org*

In considering how these can be used in a more land-focused way, I have renamed them and offer those names here:

Seed-hold Embertide occurs near the Winter Solstice. As in those older times, we will approach this practically on the little farm by making sure our seed storage is done properly: the seed for the coming planting cycle is dry and kept out of reach of mice and insects. As a spiritual observance, we will use this time to look at the coming year and make some decisions about the intentions—the seeds—we will bring into our lives as well as our practice.

Green Fire Embertide falls near the Vernal Equinox. As the life force comes out of dormancy and its period of rest, let the vigor of this time add energy to all you do. At the farm, we use this time to clear away the last of the old plantings and gardens and make way for new life, new growth. We can do the same spiritually, as we leave behind the ideas and practice—the baggage—that no longer serve us and make room for all the abundance that is to come, all based on the intentions (the seeds) we determined to plant and tend in this new cycle.

The Embertide of Tall Corn steps up at the Summer Solstice. These three days of refreshment and delight can be used to remember that life is rich and fine and much of the worry and anxiety we carry in the world shields us from the natural connection to joy. We pause in the agricultural year to enjoy the long days while also being mindful that the shift has begun to the plenty of a successful harvest. Our prayers now will include those whose lack of privilege reduces them to deprivation, and we will set our goals for alleviating suffering where we find it—even if it lies in our own souls.

Wander Days is set at the Autumnal Equinox. This Embertide is the place to unleash our imaginations and go again to our Ancestors for wisdom and help. This is the time to climb to the top of the mountain—whether literally or figuratively—and see what the wide world has to offer your soul. At the farm, we are harvesting and laying the harvest by for the Winter months. Decide now what you will rest with in the time of renewal. Contemplate the advantages of the dark and of endarkenment.

These allow us to set aside space for a deeper consideration of our spiritual lives at each of the Quarter Days, when we are already dedicated to a holy day. It is an expansion of the one-day holy day into a place that can accommodate more than one ritual, more than one gathering, and more than one meditation or prayer. There is a grace here and a generosity befitting those spiritualities that are in sync with the natural world and whose ceremonies grow out of and reflect nature's time.

Rogation Days

In Pagan circles, we sometimes talk about the holy days that were "stolen" when the Christian religion swept through tribal Europe, when it was folded into the arms of the Roman Empire. The jollification of Saturnalia translated into a celebration of the Birth of the Christ Child, and gods and demigods became peculiar saints. In addition to the Ember Days, which we have now repurposed into our Wheel of the agricultural year, we're also repurposing Rogation Day—a fascinating ceremony that coincides with the modern Earth Day in April, so is a pre-Beltane feast.

In the liturgical calendar of several branches of Christianity, Rogation Days, like Ember Days, are times of prayer, fasting, and rededication to the articles of faith, and in older times these actions were intended to bless the fields and the particular parish. Those interpretations of an earlier Roman holiday focus appropriately on the needs of the new faith, so it is interesting to dig a little more deeply and see what those crafty Romans were doing.

In the earlier iteration of this rite, the Romans were blessing the fields, too, as it turns out. The word comes from the Latin *rogare*, which means "to ask," and the festival was called the Robigalia. There was animal sacrifice, some games, and it was held in a grove outside the bounds of the city of Rome. There was a procession from the city to the site, and processions are still a part of the Christian festival in places where it is still celebrated.

The set of ceremonies allowed urban citizens to beg the gods of wild nature to spare the crops. They went out from the city center and into the countryside. They processed through fields and farmlands evoking the gods that did not live in Rome, the older gods perhaps, the ones who held the future of the harvest—and thus the future of the city—in their hands. Basically, it was the one time in the year when the city people acknowledged that the control of the state and of the burgeoning empire lay at the mercy of wild nature—anthropomorphized into divinities certainly, but not easily swayed and not to be ignored.

Several modern holidays fall around this time, and I propose we link them all together into a proper festival that incorporates Rogation Day, Arbor Day, Earth Day, and Beltane. I'm calling this "A Strange and Savage Proposal." It may indeed seem a little strange to you, but the savagery falls more in the line of willfully suggesting another change in the usual Wheel of the Year. Since we're already repurposing the Embertides and Rogation Days, I propose we lengthen the Beltane festival, arguably one of the best-loved on the Wheel of the Year anyway. I'm going to ease into that proposal by talking about two other American holidays: Arbor Day and Earth Day.

Arbor Day was first proposed by a fellow named J. Sterling Morton in 1872 in Nebraska to encourage Americans and humans everywhere to plant more trees, because trees are beautiful and they are also good windbreaks—something we will discuss later for Midsummer. There is an Arbor Day Foundation, and a donation to them or many environmental groups will garner you a bundle of free trees to plant on your property. Some states have agricultural support departments as part of the state government that do the same thing, so check with your local agriculture office and see what they have on offer.

Arbor Day is usually celebrated on April 22, which was Mr. Morton's birthday. It had been declining in popularity for some time, and now most of the Earth-loving hullaballoo is reserved for Earth Day, which was designed to fall on the same day.*

People are always surprised when I express my ambivalence about Earth Day. It came about during the ecologically troubled 1970s as a way to raise consciousness about the plight of a planet covered in debris and inhabited by people who were stripping out anything of value. This resource depletion, coupled with dead rivers and smog-filled skies, led to the creation of Earth Day, which, in turn, led to the formation of the federal Environmental Protection Agency, the National Oceanic and Atmospheric Administration, and passage of the Clean Water Act, the Endangered Species Act, and the Clean Air Act, amongst others.

Earth Day led to more changes in the psyche of American citizens. We were encouraged to conserve, to use less, to turn off the lights when we left the room. Consumers chose smaller cars, smaller houses, and learned to conserve energy by making their houses more airtight. It was a good decade, driven by passionate citizens who were led by elected officials who listened to their demands. President Jimmy Carter had solar panels installed on the White House, and it was a new day.

Then Ronald Reagan was elected president and everything began to shift. I don't need to remind you of the changes that have taken place in the last decade as Americans returned to a sense of entitlement about resources that now seem to them inexhaustible. There have been targeted rollbacks for all of the agencies and acts set in place following that first Earth Day, and Earth Day itself has changed into something unrecognizable. In my town, as in most, there is a feeble attempt at a street or stream clean-up that is poorly attended, but still a huge crowd always manages to gather downtown for the bands and the beer. There are exhibition opportunities for local green groups, with their handouts and plastic giveaway

---

* *arborday.org*

cups and visors emblazoned with logo and web address. There's at least one petition that always seems to go nowhere and everyone brings their dogs, many of whom are as difficult to be around as their children.

I woke up about ten years ago and realized what was wrong with Earth Day, at least to my way of thinking. It goes without saying that Earth Day is or should be *every day*. But I also wondered how it would feel to make it the ninth holy day on the Wheel of the Year and celebrate it with a ritual.

I called up a dozen people and asked if they'd be willing to bring a prayer, song, dance, or poem and meet me at a downtown park, the one with the big double maple tree. Almost all of them were excited about the idea. We met a few days later—on Earth Day—and honored the Earth with all those things, bringing our hearts and our souls to this holy rite.

Here's my proposal: Instead of adding a new holy day as I had originally envisioned, we weave together Rogation Day, Arbor Day, Earth Day, and Beltane and create a week-long celebration of the land, the sky, and the waters. We expand the usual one-day celebration of Beltane into a week of service, ceremony, workshops, planting, political action, and art. And we remember that the Earth is as savage and wild as ever it was as we bow, with love and humility, before that incredible power—earthquake, typhoon, volcano, avalanche, as well as the evolution process itself.

While I am treading this rambling path between folk beliefs and practices and modern Pagan holy days, I will take you with me down one more rabbit trail. There are two European holidays that have much to tell us about how those people lived, the lives they built, what was important to them, and what frightened them. These are practiced in several different cultures, so if your Ancestors hail from a particular place with a strong tradition of either of these celebrations, you will want to look to those practices, those myths, and those stories.

Both come from earlier Christian traditions, and both have connections not only to the land but also to the spirits of the land and to the spirits of the dead. Michaelmas and Martinmas have some things we can glean for the expansion of our own practices, and they are also tied into our agrarian roots.

Michaelmas has come down to us as a special time to honor the Archangels and specifically Michael. Michael is a popular figure amongst Catholic, Orthodox, and Anglican Christians as well as many Pagans. Michaelmas is associated with acts of wonder and magic and with feasting, primarily on goose. Folklore also tells us that blackberries—and really any brambles—must not be picked after Michaelmas, in some cases because the Devil spits on them and in others because they must be left for the land spirits. Archangel Michael is said to protect his devotees from darkness and evil, which leads me to think that honoring those beings that protect us is not bad thing, whether they are in the form of an Archangel or not. We can use this time at the end of September when the nights grow steadily longer to acknowledge the various protections bestowed on us and to beseech Divines and other spirits to be with us in times of need when we are at our most vulnerable.

Martinmas is another thing altogether. It is the feast day of St. Martin of Tours, who was not at all favorable to Pagan religions. Its older focus was the final harvest and the slaughter of herd animals as they were brought in fattened up from the Summer pastures. It is celebrated on November 11 (Armistice Day) and sometimes referred to as Old Hallowe'en.

This was also a time for weather prognostication. According to folklore, if the weather is warm on St. Martin's Day, then a harsh Winter will follow: conversely, if the weather at Martinmas is icy, then Christmas will be bright and warmer than usual.

In many areas, the winter wheat was sown at Martinmas. Wine and cider had fermented and were ready to enjoy. Martinmas is often celebrated with processions, especially by lantern-light. And there is another interesting tie-in to Samhain, and the clue is in its occasional designation as Old Hallowe'en. Martinmas is a time when the dead return, as either spirit beings or reanimated corpses. An old song "The Wife of Usher's Well" features a grieving mother calling her sons back from the dead through her unrelenting sorrow. The sons return at Martinmas, but they aren't quite right and must return to the world of the dead following their farewell visit home.

CHAPTER THREE

A Different Means to Reckon Time

Wake, Work, Wonder, and Sleep

Outside the window, the steady wind wriggles the dried oak leaves that have clung to their connectors through much of the Winter. Both the oak and its stout companion the witch hazel refuse to release last year's leaves until they are sure that Spring is indeed in the offing. They linger there after the colors of Fall have released themselves into the soil of the compost pile, after the reds, golds, and oranges give up the final vestiges of their former lives, pounded by rain, pressed by snow.

If they contain a sense of time, it is not one governed by clock or calendar. Sap rising again into the sharpest branches and twigs signals these lingerers as sure as if a church tower bell has rung the hours. One by one they release (and are released), and the woodland changes. Awaited freedom leading to change is a simplistic metaphor for human engagement in the Anthropocene, but it is an apt one. We want to look at the uses of time in the natural world and the ways in which the human component of the ancient land can reintegrate into a multiphase system for reckoning time.

Day and Night

We have been on the land all day, reweaving the hedge, turning the new compost. Our supper was a thick stew, with warm bread and butter, washed down with a homebrew laid down a few months back. We've played some music on the porch, washed our faces, and brushed our teeth. Time to begin our day.

We've had too much coffee at our cubicle job, and we're drinking water on the train that takes us home. There's a stop to make at the deli for a grab-and-go salad and a turkey wrap. Then it's in the door of the little apartment building, picking up the mail in the lobby and heading upstairs in the slow elevator. Balancing all our stuff, we unlock the door and bend precariously to greet the silly dog. We watch the news, put on our pajamas, and start the day.

We have been tidying and picking up all day while nursing a cranky sick child. Supper is simple, and the older children are cajoled into homework, then nightwear, and finally bed. A quiet cup of herbal tea and a quick check of social media, laughing at a meme with goats and cats. Last-minute dishes washed, we get into bed, and tomorrow arrives as we pull up the blankets.

Each of these three similar scenarios has the same surprise ending. The leaves had something to teach us after all—more than a sentimental meme. The decision to begin your day in the darkness has become important for many people who are recreating their expression of time. When you begin your day with rest and darkness, you invite sleep to be an active part of all that you do, instead of the deadened end of a long day. When the day ends as you turn off the bedside lamp and begins as you engage the process of rest-into-sleep, a couple of things happen. You start your day gently and slowly, able to access the knowledge that waits for you in your dream life. The day starts with the possibilities of engaging with your imaginative interior and gives that portion of your life a new significance. The sound of the alarm a few hours later signals the change in your day from rest to physical activity—but your day began in rest and continues from that base. Does this alter the way your twenty-four-hour expression of time looks from the outside? Not at all. There is a span of activity and wakefulness and a shorter one of rest and less activity.

The change is in our interior selves, in the place where our brains and souls travel through a potentially mythic landscape. We begin to incorporate the night and the act of dreaming, folding them into the possibilities of the entire "day." Dawning, rising, and physical movement are an extension of the night, bringing mystery and dream into the fullness of our everyday enchanted lives.

In the Night Season: Sleep, Rest, Dream

When we begin our day at sundown and recognize the value of such a start to the day, the realm of night—the Night Season—becomes filled with delight and possibility. We can restructure our attitude as well as our schedule.

We set up our day with a good meal and acts of self-care (brushed teeth, clean face), and we put on the appropriate clothing. We set our intention for the next seven or eight hours and perform those small acts that will make this time more manageable—plug the phone in to charge and set the alarm. Instead of getting into the car or heading for the bus stop, we kick off our shoes and get into bed.

Days of Wonder and Twilight Miracles

We settle in, leaving behind the bewilderments of the day. *Bewilderment*— the word intrigued me so I spent some time with it, and its roots were what I suspected: "to go astray, to wander, to lose your way." Because I love words, I took it a bit farther. It is the first step in our return to these acknowledged kinships I am striving to learn and to teach. When we have gone far from our usual turf in the natural world and its honest rawness begins to call us home, we may balk at first. We may even be afraid and unwilling, though the step back is tempting us. Let us consider that bewilderment is a portal through which we walk backwards, sensing rather than seeing the return trip to our wild selves. It is a state of mind and of spirit that takes clear sight and an open heart to push through.

When we leave bewilderment behind as head touches pillow, we allow our dream-worlds to show us pathways our conscious minds and our cultures have forbidden us. As our breathing becomes more regular and we come to the dreaming place in the Night Season, we allow ourselves to begin the day with a powerful and regenerative lesson in homecoming.

If we accept the idea that time is not linear, then so many other interesting ways of shaping our concepts of it are possible. The Wheel can be divided in any number of ways. One way was the choice of some European tribes: a division into two parts feels navigable. Summer moves to Winter and cycles back to Summer again. The rainy season is followed by the time of growing, harvesting, and preserving, which is followed by the rainy season. These two big divisions can be thought of as hinges in the Wheel that allow us to open the structure and step inside for a more detailed observation of smaller pieces in order to make the whole thing more human-sized and accessible.

I will argue throughout this book for a return to a human scale within our human lives. In the old Scandinavian tale that has come down to us, courtesy of Peter Christen Asbjørnsen and Jørgen Moe, as "East of the Sun, West of the Moon," a brave girl seeks to correct a wrong she committed and must travel through forests and over mountains until she arrives at the place where she can save her love. She trades in a golden apple and a golden carding comb and a golden spinning wheel, but the thing that saves him and gives the couple their happily ever after is that she reverses the mess she made in the first place by cleaning the tallow from his shirt. She moves through the whole wide world only to find the simple act of cleaning a shirt is the thing that works. She manages the unmanageable by moving through and with time and with small, simple acts that add up to her success.

CHAPTER FOUR

Re-Enchantment and the Uses of Magic

The woods that make up the bulk of the forest-farm take up a narrow strip that is a third as wide as it is long. It is bordered on one side with an access road to the back of the property and on the other side with the backyards of two neighbors. Before I owned the property, there was a fence along that side, but it has since fallen to ruin, as untended wire fences tend to do.

In the middle of the woods there is an old poplar that stretches above much of the canopy. It drops its yellow tulip flowers in the Spring, and in its branches the neighborhood crow family is often heard perching and fussing. There are three members of this corvid tribe that seem to have adopted us and scream happily when one or both of our cars are there. We want to feed them but haven't quite worked out how to do that without also feeding the rats, the raccoons, and the bear.

We were sitting on the porch one afternoon, discussing business and plotting how to deal with the shade in the front of the house, when a young deer came bounding out of the woods, leapt through the side and then the front yard, and was gone into the neighboring woods across the road.

There are bluebirds here, usually spotted in the small garden area directly behind the house. They turn up every Spring, and it never fails to delight us and give us the feeling of imminent good fortune.

So much about this place is magical, in the contemporary sense of that word. It is a charming cottage set back from the road with oak and holly trees standing all around. The neighbors still consider it a "witch's" house and warn newcomers not to disturb us, though we haven't had an outdoor ritual there in over a decade. The memories of Saturday coven meetings in the woods have lingered with the oldest inhabitants, and they obviously feel the need to pass on their knowledge.

Ours is a place where the scent of magic still lingers in the little wood, where old stories have set their seal on the place. All the world is the same, you know. The scent of old magic lingering amidst the highways and skyscrapers, leaking out of the thousand-acre cornfields of the Midwest, peering over the edges of mesas. In the times before our times—mostly easily found now in faery tales and legends—magic was as tangible as dew. It was used by all sorts of folks: priests and midwives, children and elders. Magic was felt in the everyday, with only high magic reserved for the most significant occasions.

In some places, this native and lively magic is still observed and tangible. Most of us can recall a place where we felt something of the old sizzle of magic "in the air." But so much of the world now feels mechanized and impersonal, and it has led many people to believe that magic is only stage illusion and not at all real. Magic then becomes the province of children and cosplayers, and the rest of us are left feeling the loss.

It is possible to re-enchant the modern world, and it is basically a simple process. Like bringing poisoned Tinker Bell back from the brink of death in *Peter Pan*, we can choose—intentionally choose—to believe in magic again.

There are people who scoff at the sort of "magical thinking" at the heart of re-enchantment processes: they know without a doubt that influencing what is happening in your world by the power of your intention is simply not possible. To publicly acknowledge a belief in magical thinking is to open yourself to the concerned and sometimes mocking advice of those around you. And I confess to a belt-and-suspenders philosophy about much of my personal magical practice—to do the practical thing in conjunction with intention may be the way to ensure the most success.

I offer a class in simple practical magic for beginners that also acts as a refresher course for those with more experience. As a witch who practices folk magic, my approach is as described in the title: simple and practical. We spend more time on grounding, centering, and accessing energy than we do copying spells, and everyone is encouraged to find something simple that they consistently need—like parking, which is especially helpful in busy downtowns. Several parking spells are discussed with the advice to find one that works for that practitioner. The proof of the pudding is, of course, in the eating, and I encourage them to be scientists and test their work as best they can. If something works once, try it three more times and see what your results are. If it doesn't work, keep experimenting with words and energy patterns until you find an alignment that works for you.

Magical practice invites us to approach this work as scientists do: confirm our conclusions, do blind testing, and experiment with various ways to achieve the desired end. Practice is essential for a consistent result, and students are encouraged to enhance their daily lives with these uses of magic and to refrain from saving them for a rainy day. Without consistent practice and repetition, we won't be effective when the clouds open up.

But re-enchantment is not simply the practice of magic. It is also returning to a sense of the foundational animism in our world, to a change not only in how we experience the natural world but also how we view it and our place in it. If every stone and tree is ensouled, we are offered a chance to return to the childlike delight of the things all around us.

In our complex modern world, we often talk about the importance of relationship *with* and relationship *to* any number of things—so much so that the meaning and significance of the word *relationship* often become lost in the width of its use. In pondering how profoundly we are affected by the embrace of an animistic worldview, I have searched for language that more clearly expresses that idea and came up with this—*acknowledged kinship*.

Like the word *love*, we use *relationship* to describe an attachment as narrow as the one with our favorite bank teller, the bond between us and our child, and any other connections physical, emotional, and collegial between ourselves and others. Because it has such a breadth of meaning, the word is in constant use. And a noun used in so many circumstances for so many things soon loses a solid meaning and real definition. It is then necessary to step back from it and decide what we truly convey when we employ it. Intention—another overused word, especially in the Pagan community—and thought are helpful tools as we sharpen the world around us and within us with the terms we use to describe it.

In this effort to reconnect humans to the natural world from which we find ourselves estranged, I considered both the rebuilding of bonds and the causes for the initial parting of ways. It is easy enough to blame the language of Genesis and the subsequent empire of Christianity for this separation, but few things are as simple as that. The natural world is dangerous to an animal that doesn't possess defensive claws, envenomed fangs, or armored skin. To ensure survival, humans are smart to assemble ourselves in tribes or family units that can protect the weaker and older members of the group. As we became primarily farmers and left behind much of our gathering and hunting lifestyle, humans relied more and more on our multifaceted and large brains, but we never really forgot the fear of being hunted—of being prey rather than predator. The world outside our walls and fences was one of half-remembered terror. As our civilizations moved forward, those same walls and fences also held our own species at bay. In our lust for resources—land, gold, safety, souls—the *world outside* came to include those others who were not of our tribe or lineage. The old laws of hospitality became strained and honored more in the breach than the attendance.

But we never left nature; we just redefined our relationship to it. Humans as the dominant—the alpha—species never could escape the land that fed us, the waters that transported us, the weather that tormented us. So we reframed that bond. We were the stewards of the land— superior to it, even as we were bound to it. We were to wrest our living from the sweat of our brows, taken from the earth by force, subduing and repressing it with the sheer might of our will. We will reframe it again, here in the opening gambit of the Anthropocene, as global climate shift and resource inequality finally become mainstream topics.

I propose that we remember that older bonding when we were a clever and invasive species. I propose we look at this relationship for what it really is: a complicated series of connections, this symbiotic and acknowledged kinship with all things.

How do we do this, practice animism? What are the practical steps to finding a place of acknowledged kinship with the world around us? We'll look at steps and processes, confident that we large-brained and creative humans can come to such a place, such a change in where and what we are.

Here are some small but significant processes you may consider as you do this work, listed in no particular order:

Slow down and occasionally stop. Watch your hands as you lock your front door. Look at the sky and note clouds. It has become a truism in modern culture that we are moving too fast, have no time, use busy-ness as an excuse for non-engagement. This leads us to lives nearly unlived as we move frantically from one thing to another. To take one minute out of your frantic pace may simply feel impossible. This doesn't have to be the first step, but it is an important one and will lead us to better observation and a widening sense of self in connection with the world around us.

Don't shut yourself off, out of exhaustion and fear. No, you can't add another thing to your life. You are too tired and feel too vulnerable, and it— whatever *it* is—doesn't feed your family or advance you in your career.

You have learned that keeping your shields up serves you very well and you haven't had to deal with other people's rank emotional sewerage. Sometimes, given the world in which many of us function, this is the only way to survive to the end of your week. You can ease yourself in by observing when you are in a place of relative safety and remembering that opening yourself to the energies and vitality of the world around you will actually help you and add to your internal stores.

Delight in impermanence. As you solidify your ability to observe changes around you in a way that doesn't frighten you or make you anxious, it may be important to remind yourself that all things have a season and to find as much joy in the grape hyacinths as they bloom as you do in the photo you posted of them in your social media account. Delighting in impermanence gives us all a leg-up in dealing with change—which is inevitable, but doesn't have to be hurtful.

Practice slow-seeing. It can also be called small-seeing. We are encouraged by the dominant culture to see the "big picture," which helps with planning long term but can lead us to think that subtleties and common things don't have as much to teach us and therefore have less value. As you get into your car, take a moment before you close the door to look at the world that will be outside in a moment. Note the sky, the ground; look through the windshield and towards the horizon.

Collect small beauties. This collecting can be picking up small rocks or honoring the beauty of the spider web near your car. Sometimes we collect experiences and hold them in our hearts and memories, and that is certainly enough. Instead of cluttering one more shelf with things you never look at but only dust, consider holding those small beauties in photos and in the heart of your memory.

Use your imagination and a well-developed sense of wonder. If you were a toddler, we wouldn't be discussing this. You would wander through your world with an expectation of adventure and newness. You'd have no idea what waits for you around the corner, and you might imagine it is a dragon or a dog or an eagle with balloons—all of which would make you gasp and clap your hands. As adults, we tend to use our imaginations to conjure the worst-case scenario for even the smallest challenge—often at three in the morning. This is partly due to years of experience. But it also denotes an imagination funk that can, and to my way of thinking should, be corrected. Provoking anxiety, borrowing trouble—try to let those things fall away as you consider the kindly and beneficial possibilities of the path you walk.

Stop telling yourself that this is silly and unimportant. Unless you are one of the people who are fortunate in your home, work, and social circles, you may encounter all sorts of resistance to the magical thinking this book invites you to. There may be gentle amusement at your childlike view on the world, which is easy enough to step back from. You may be met with some scorn and smart remarks. None of that matters as you reacquaint yourself with the world you inhabit, one leaf at a time.

Abide in silence. This may be the most difficult of all for those of us who can hear, but also the most important. Our world is not quiet. Even if you abide, as we do, on a small forest-farm, there is always sound: human-made sound, animal and bird sound, wind through trees sound, rain on roof sound. Silence then becomes a state of mind—as we found with bewilderment—that we actively enter into to learn what is kept from us by the wall of noises that we inhabit. Silence can signal danger, as it often does in the natural world. Silence is part of death. In these ways silence is more than turning off the phone and shutting your mouth. It gives us the opportunity to alter our consciousness in such a way that we open our souls to a different sort of integrated experience.

A Stone, a Leaf: Leaving and Returning to Mundania

For some Pagans, the few months of the festival season hold more than a chance to see old friends, attend rituals and ceremonies with a like-minded congregation, and indulge in other favorite activities, like camping and bonfires, drumming and dancing—all the things that may be more difficult to enjoy at home base. Volunteers greet new arrivals with "Welcome home!" And Sunday afternoons find those same people breaking down camp, saying their good-byes, and dismally approaching the imminent return to what is called "Mundania."

I can't think of a better way to minimize our lives—to feel bereft and resentful. Certainly vacation time is a time set apart from most of our lives, and that gives it a special feel. It is the idea that we spend the majority of our year in a place where we abide but can't actually live our authentic lives, which is deeply problematical. This kind of thinking encourages us to put our lives on hold and to consider time a burden instead of a gift. All those moments then get lost to boredom and anxiety as we wait to rejoin "our" people so we can be fully alive.

We cannot reconnect to the natural world while still intentionally disconnecting ourselves from most of our lives. Reframe, renew. You needn't wear long black robes and a pentacle the size of a salad plate to practice an authentic and meaningful spirituality. There is no reason for any of us to compromise our beliefs—we may simply have to internalize those beliefs and act upon them. When you consider every inch of the Earth as a sacred and sentient life-form of which you are a dynamic part—and if you really believe it, instead of echoing the popular sentiment of the day—you spend time differently.

If you are confused and frightened, still yourself and listen to nature. Listen to the wind, to the waking trees, to the birds as they sing out their boundaries.

Hear the voices of your Ancestors as they whisper their stories. As they whisper to us to be strong, to be smart, to look beyond the obvious and the ordinary.

Follow the land spirits as they lead us to the edges and the hedgerows, the places where magic is hatched. Touch the land with your fingertips. Drum the pulse of the waking earth.

Feel the magic in your fingertips move up through your arms, into your shoulders, throughout your body and enter your heart.

Take a breath. One more. One more. Reside in communicative silence.

Now, release that magic back into the world—into your house and your neighborhood, into your city and country, your state, your nation, the widest world.

Let that be your work as the seasons change—to re-enchant the world. Re-enchant the world by touching your fingertips to the earth.

And so it is.

CHAPTER FIVE

The Good Neighbors, the Land Spirits

In a land inspirited, with an animism worldview, there is no Veil.

Much of modern Pagan practice has emphasized an energetic boundary between the worlds of matter and spirit, between the human world and the Otherworld. In many areas in North America, this Veil began to slip at the Winter Solstice of 2009—in some places earlier than that, in some places later. We began to experience unexplained phenomena—a colleague remembers seeing a glowing bird that was otherworldly and how that experience opened him to other observed events. That story is repeated again and again, so many times that I have come to ask new acquaintances about any experiences they may have had. Some of these have been related to non-human spirits of the sort we have come to call the Fae, the Seelie and Unseelie, the Sidhe and the Good Neighbors. Others are experiencing a new connection with their spirit-kin: the ghosts of Ancestors and friends who find the passage between our worlds to be easier than it was before. Some of this may be related to a resurgence in Ancestor veneration in the West, as well as a deepening belief in the existence of spirits and Divinities outside the purview of the globally dominant Abrahamic faiths.

Over the Borderlands and into the Realms

When I teach about these subjects, the language I use to describe the places and the activities differs from what you might usually hear. I refer to the boundaries between us and them as *the Borderlands*, and the lands beyond that porous layer I dub *the Realms*. In my experience through meditation and conscious dreamwork, there is more than one place over in "Faery-land," and I desire, above all things in this work, to be consistent and unfailingly polite. I do not assume that everyone gets along with everyone else, and I never presume that they are like us, either culturally or physically. I always start from the position that my presence in their country is not welcome and the unexpected should always be expected. There are many books for you to consider and peruse on this subject, of varying degrees of quality and scholarship. I have found that my best sources have been close readings of folk and faery tales. The keys often lie in stories we heard as children, told so often that we've forgotten the importance of welcoming the stranger, sharing your meal with the peculiar traveler you meet along your journey, and following the taboos in the creepy castle exactly as the stories said. Contracts and bargains are never a good idea. Don't take any food or drink that is offered you, but reject it in a way that does not cause offence. Working with and for them is not something to enter into lightly. That being said, here is where the rules of engagement are changing too fast to ken as the people who live there have information we need to heal and liberate the planet and our sad little species, too.

Genius Loci

The definition of this term *genius loci* has changed since it was first employed by the Romans. Now, we think of the spirit of a place as its vibe, its personality and what it's known for culturally. Anyone who has been there knows that New York *feels* different from Chicago, and Bay St. Louis isn't the same as Charleston. In the built environment this has to do with the topography of the land as well as its geographic location and the architecture that dominates the skyline. In a natural setting, it is often easier to fathom. The Smoky Mountains are not the same as the Sierra Madre. The Ohio River is not the Missouri.

The Romans thought of a genius loci quite differently. To them, actual beings—gods and demigods—dwelt in particular places, in many cases acting as protectors, as guardians of that place. They are anthropomorphized as strong-limbed women in soft robes, often bearing cornucopias, branches of fruit trees, and other symbols of prosperity and abundance. These entities are both numinous and tutelary—*numinous* being a quality of place that suggests the presence of unseen divine spirits and *tutelary* describing the spirit itself, divine or quasi-divine, that is the protector or historic patron/matron of a place, culture, or family. A genius loci is an example of a tutelary being, and the place it protects may be described as numinous.

I have often written that there are places I have experienced that are *spirit-haunted landscapes*, a phrase I borrowed from Flannery O'Connor, then tweaked a bit to serve my requirements.* Whether those places are literally haunted by the ghosts of humans past or if there are spirits attached to the land may be hard to determine. But many people can feel the presence of spirit—often described as a "fizziness" in the air, like bubbles in sparkling water.

Humans enjoy ranking things—smallest to largest, lightest to heaviest, least important to most important—and spirits are often ranked by power and influence. Hierarchical rankings are not particularly helpful, in my experience, whether you are dealing with the spirit world or a new book club. I prefer to deal with situations and the people in them one by one and to learn as much as I can about likes and dislikes, as well as individual history in a place or role. This has served me well in the physical

---

*Flannery O'Connor made a startling observation about herself and her fellow Southerners: "By and large," she said, "people in the South still conceive of humanity in theological terms. While the South is hardly Christ-centered, it is most certainly Christ-haunted. The Southerner who isn't convinced of it is very much afraid that he may have been formed in the image and likeness of God" (from Mystery and Manners: Occasional Prose, posthumous).

world as well as the spiritual one, and I often bring it to bear when puzzling out who is who, where they bide, and if it is safe to approach.

The beings that I am most fond of are the ones I have experienced for much of my life: our genii loci, the ones I refer to as the Cousins. These are the indigenous land spirits of this region—beings that have made themselves known to inhabitants here for centuries. They have taught me so much about themselves and the land, and they have taught it with a gentle humor. Through trial and error, I have learned that the Cousins do not want butter, cream, and fresh bread. They prefer brightly colored candies with flavors as startling as their colors, too-sweet alcohol, and bits of shiny glass.

Ancestors

Ancestor veneration is nothing new—except in the West, where we lost these practices for many generations. Now many groups are reinventing the renewal of these old bonds. Memorial shrines, Ancestor altars, cemetery visitations, and the study of family trees through genealogy are some of these incarnations. I have used guided meditation and trance to access those Eldest, the ones we can trace through our family lineages. Here is one example of the results of such a trance journey:

You stand on a stony beach, the smooth rocks digging into your bare feet. The rhythmic breathing begins, slowing, deepening. Breath lifting, each intake of air a buoyance, filling your lungs until your lungs fill your entire body. The air inside you is so light and your body rises into the cool evening air. You rise upright, the stony beach receding below your feet. You rise above the tree line and bend your body westward. The land below you is darkening, settling towards night. But there is still enough light to see the tended fields and the farmer bringing her cows to the byre. The crows call their families home to the branches and your journey takes you farther still, over a great forest of pines. You see mountains on the horizon and know they are your ultimate destination. The sky continues to darken, the first stars appear above and around you, and still you fly, the night going velvet around you.

The mountains are barely visible now, but your inner navigation knows home and you slow in your flight, your feet pointing to the land below, suddenly heavy, weighing you down to the earth again. Landing lightly, you exhale a long stream, fogging the cold mountain air. You look around the small plateau and give yourself time, time to reconnect to the earth. A few steps away a rough stair winds its way up the face of the mountain. It's carved from the mountain, a tumbled heap of blocks that lead upward, almost too big to step up and onto.

But you manage somehow, stretching your legs as far as they can, block by block. Your nose catches the smell of bread and of roasting meat. Your belly growls and you climb a little faster. As you peer upward into the dark, you detect a faint glow and suspect the good smells originate there. At last your striving is rewarded and you stand on the top of the last block before walking slowly towards the warmth.

They are there, as they always are and always have been. Seated around a central fire on a ledge protruding over the gorge are the Eldest ones, the Ancestors of the Ancestors. The smell of food is tantalizing but you hang back, watching, waiting. Your head reaches only as far as shoulder height of the nearest one and that person is seated. Its clothes are roughly tex-tured and layered, some animal fur and woven wool, every shade of green and grey, the colors of forest and stone. The nearest one turns to you at last and gestures you forward. There is a seat for you, padded with a soft cloth. You sit, a child at the grown-ups' table, and a wooden bowl is passed to you, with chunks of meat swimming in broth. You watch the others, as they tip similar bowls to their mouths to drink the broth then use their wide fingers to pick out pieces of the tender meat and pop them into their mouths. There are laughter and stories, as they wipe their mouths and demand more bread and more stew.

You are in this strange old place to listen and to hear—to listen to the voices, the songs, the poetry and to hear the wisdom that slips easily from these great hoary heads. Nothing is asked of you but to observe the rules of hospitality, to eat with these Eldest, and to open your ears wide. You smile at the thought of widening your ears and the ones across the fire see you and slap their thighs and laugh, pointing at your expressive mirth. You have seldom felt such kinship, so profound a sense of belonging.

The night is almost done. The bird sounds have changed. You rise from your seat and praise the Eldest with poem and song, thanking them for all they are and were and will be. You move to the edge of the circle with the fire at your back and you breathe as before. Your lungs fill with air, your body slowly rises up from the surface. You turn back once and then you rise above the ledge and the Eldest, tilting your body forward to face the east. You fly away from the mountains as the sky moves from black to dark grey, as the stars fade into the birth of the morning. Below is the great pine forest and the farmer coming out of her warm house to do the milking. The crow family flies from the limbs of the trees and far below a rooster crows the Sun up, making the land pink and gold. You come back to the stony beach and your heavy feet weigh you downwards until your toes feel the roundness of the pebbles there. Firm in your footing, the Sun lighting your path, you exhale into the last of the glistening mist and turn from the beach for home.

These beings of spirit and mist that inhabit the land in which we humans bide are a part of these webs of being we are exploring. They also inhabit our mythic world, our imaginations filled with their ineffable presence and their seductive parallel worlds. Stepping into these webs, into this weaving of time, land, and life, we come to a wholeness that was thought forever lost. With our interwoven lives now acknowledged as the deepest kinship, we can study the cycle of seasonal celebration, spiritual endeavors, and work on a human scale that we have come to call the Wheel of the Year. Come with me now to explore the year as lived on a small forest-farm.

Part Two

The Wheel of the Agricultural Year

The year unfolds in simple and lovely ways at our small forest-farm. There is always work to be done, and each season brings its own particular chores to do and skills to hone. It's the same the world over, whether you are on the edge of the woods or surrounded by high-rises. Still, making the space for wonder, for slow-seeing, for abiding within the weave of our days opens up the magic in common things and the small beauties that surround us. Sharing in community with neighbors seen and unseen forges connections to our place and creates the spirit of a home.

Now we come to the festivals, the celebrations and the simple acts of living that make up the Wheel of the Agricultural Year. After our studies of time, acknowledged kinship, and the interconnected webs of being, join us at the small forest-farm for a turning from Winter to Winter and all the ways these transformative seasons unfold through the work of heart and hand. Whether you are working a smallholding in the country, spending your days in a cubicle in the city, or abide in one of the places in between, you are welcome to experience the enchantment and plain work that connect us.

CHAPTER SIX

Winter:
The Waxing Year

Samhain

Winter Solstice

Imbolc

Vernal Equinox

1

The Season of Samhain, Summer's Ending

Holy, silent, end of year
Ancestors and land spirits gather near.
The final harvest here at last
Winter coming much too fast.
Turnips hollowed to lend light
Show our way on Samhain night.

Letter from the Forest-Farm: Seated at Summer's End

GOOD EVENING TO YOU ALL from the very edge of the little wood. We are washing canning jars and eating the last of the previous year's frozen produce before the inevitable freezer burn makes it inedible. The harvest-time on any smallholding brings so much work, some fear or anxiety, and a dollop of pure joy. We head towards the old year's demise surrounded by delicious things to eat, many of which have to be processed and preserved, and we have a weather eye on the coming of Winter with all it entails.

Many places in the world shapeshift from the green of late Summer to an ever-changing and eye-popping color palette depending on how many trees make their home in the region and have been allowed to live, in spite of human encroachment and development. The color change starts slowly and usually with the sunny yellow and gold of maple trees, followed immediately by another maple's orange blaze. The mountain above the farm goes from a dusty and tired green to startling flashes of color until the flanks of the mountains have transformed into fire.

These may be the last weeks of fine weather, and it is wise to use them as you need. But don't only put your head down and your shoulder to the wheel and miss out on the passing into Autumn—those moments (or days!) that find you wandering in the mountains filling your eyes and your soul, a necessity as we approach the grey days of Winter.

If there is a need and a strange compulsion towards "Spring cleaning," there is an equal tug in the Fall of the year, and we should give tidying especially some good attention. If you decorate for Hallowe'en, Thanksgiving, and the Yuletide, you would do well to clear some space now and avoid the frustration of boxing up all those bookshelf and mantel extras to make room. Be sure to label tubs and boxes—we always think we will remember what we put in that obnoxiously colored tub, but we rarely do. A stout black marker and some old-fashioned masking tape will do you a world of good.

Your wooden furniture will benefit from a good dusting and some polishing, too. If you live in a place where you must heat your house come Winter, giving it a coating of good-quality polish will help it stay beautiful.

My Good-Smelling Polish

In the top of a double boiler, put about five ounces of olive oil, an ounce of beeswax (chopped or pellets), and a quarter teaspoon (or less) of lemon essential oil. Put water in the bottom part of the double boiler and heat it gently (stirring with a wooden spoon) until it all comes together, then pour into a heavy jar with a good lid. It smells nice while it's making. Let it cool. To use—apply a small amount with a soft cloth and rub it vigorously (as though you are giving that old china closet a massage) and enjoy both the sight and the smell of your work.

The season from the Autumn Equinox until now, when we set ourselves to look backwards to those who have died since the previous Samhain and to honor the Beloved Dead from the Long Past, is a time of great reflection, as we will cover in the chapter on that sacred time of preparation and the delights of the Second Harvest. You will have spent some time making things right in your world by apologizing to those you've wronged in some way; you've paid back money you owed as you've been able and gotten your house in order. This way you enter into Winter with a clean slate and a clear heart.

This is the dreaming season, too. Take a moment in the morning to jot down a few notes about your dreams the night before and consider what they may mean. In my part of the world, many people have precognitive or prophetic dreams, and we always listen to them when they surprise us with an early morning call or text message. If you have trouble remembering your dreams, this is a good time to try out different bedtime routines until you find one that allows you to easily get to the deep sleep required for them.

Some of us were cautioned or even punished for daydreaming, especially while in school, church, or other locales where we were supposed to be paying attention. Creative people need that outlet, and this time of year can easily find us watching the changing sky, resting our eyes on distant colors, and dreaming improbable dreams that might well become intentions for the coming cycle.

We'll fill our pockets with some dreams and notions and carry them about us as we face our Ancestors and the Beloved Dead. For this is their time, this final harvest. Now is the time we perform the ancient and sacred duties and offer the hospitality that is their right.

Samhain invites us to grasp the chalice of grief and to drink in memories—the sharp, difficult as well as the tender ones. These days have come down to us as the time of saints and souls for a reason. Establishing strong ties with our spirit kindred—those of blood and bone and those our hearts have called—is the primal strand that connects us to the land and to our personal and familial myth. The little farm and its little forest form the crucible in which the work of heart, hand, and spirit can commence.

Skills

Storytelling: Family Lore and Its Keepers

I come from and live within a culture that honors and cherishes its storytellers, its tale-makers. There are professionals who compete at festivals; there are "liars' benches"—informal gatherings of people who try to outdo each other in telling the tallest, most impossible tale, all while swearing it is perfectly true. But everyone here is a natural teller, and we will take the simplest story and weave it into a piece of strange performance art.

We are not alone in this. There is something comforting and enchanting about this ability to craft everyday life into a place of story, and people the world over do it. It is another way to re-enchant the places all around us and to dispel—slowly but surely—the notion of a mundane world.

Before there were devices to entertain and delight us at the push of a button, humans craved news and gossip to take their minds off the uncertainty and grief that are an inevitable part of our lives. But there was so much work to do, most of the time, that we set aside the evening and the time after our work to relate these pieces of history that give the family a sense of who they are, what it is.

From Samhain until the Winter Solstice, we can practice telling stories of our current lives and remembering what the children said and did when they were smaller. Then the stories morph to the previous generation and how these children behave much like that particular—and maybe peculiar—Ancestor. With each tale we dig more deeply into the heart of the family, and we establish ourselves in a woven-together world that we are creating.

The perpetual obsession with our ancestry and places of origin adds fuel to this warming fire of tales and also gives us new settings to try out. Highwayman, serving-woman, enslaved person, priest—all people our imagination and set the course for possibilities, for hope, for reclamation.

Tending the Dying and the Dead

Samhain is a time when we take particular care to honor those who have passed from matter to spirit so it seems a good place to discuss end-of-life issues and the practical matters of tending to the dying and the dead.

We will get the paperwork out of the way first. Create end-of-life documents for yourself now and encourage your family and everyone you know to do the same. There are readily available forms online that can be filled out with an hour of careful uninterrupted thought. You'll need most of the following: a will, a power of attorney, a health care power of attorney, advance directive/Living Will/Five Wishes Planner, DNR/DNI order, organ donor designation, and a list of who gets what of your belongings. There are other things that you'll want to account for if you want your magical tools and paraphernalia distributed or taken care of a particular way. Write it down. Invite your friends over for snacks and drinks and spend the evening designing your funeral. And write that down too.

When we do these things, we accomplish a couple of important jobs. We let those who outlive us know exactly what we want so they don't have to be grieving your loss while trying to read your mind. It makes it easier on them. Even if you don't give a fig about what happens to your things and your body, write that down. You will need an attorney for some of this, so go ahead and get that done.

You will want to revisit these documents periodically to see if everything still fits. Pick a day you won't forget, like your birthday or New Year's Day. It isn't hard, won't take a lot of time, and becomes a gift to your friends and family. The point is to make those decisions now.

There are groups in every good-sized community who will help you through these processes. There are now death doulas and end-of-life midwives who also regularly do this powerful and beautiful work. Avail yourself of their services and see what is available as far as green burials, cremation, and other options for your body and those of your loved ones. Find out what is legal in your area and what is required. Many of the arbitrary rules have been lifted, and you will find flexibility in most end-of-life matters. Shop around for a casket, if you want one, or build your own while you're strong enough to do it. Choose a beautiful handmade cookie jar for your ashes.

More people are choosing to die at home, and you'd be wise to check out the rules around that in your area. Handmade funerals are gaining in popularity, and preparing the body of someone you love is a powerful final service, a gift to yourself and those who assist with the preparation. The end-of-life community can coach you on how to proceed, and there are also websites and books to help.

Consider a shroud. It sounds mad, doesn't it? But I know several people who have created the shrouds that will wrap them on the final journey. One friend—who was expected to die for several years—asked his friends and wife to make a shroud for him and he'd wrap up in it to watch TV in the evening.

Chores

Fallen Leaves

If you can possibly resist it, refrain from raking up fallen leaves until you do your clean-up in the Spring. The leaves will begin to break down and add their nutrients to your soil. The debris will give beneficial insects and other creatures a place to overwinter, too. This is not always possible, especially if you live in the sort of community that has rules about what you can and can't do with your yard. If that is the case, tidy up as you are required and make sure and roll around in the leaves before you bag or compost them. Speaking of compost, if you don't have space to compost leaves or kitchen scraps, check your community to see if there's a group that offers this service.

It is smart to wait until the majority of the leaves have fallen or you'll have to do it all again. Raking is very good exercise, so you may choose to keep the lawn tidy and rake once a week. That choice is entirely up to you. The lightweight rake with splayed tines is called a leaf rake and sometimes a leaf broom. I prefer one with metal tines but the plastic ones are almost as good—though they seem to need replacing more often than the metal ones.

Water Catchment

A rain barrel used to be a common sight and the concept of water catchment has certainly made a comeback in recent years. Any sizeable garden center will have options for rain collecting kits, and they are simple enough to construct from scratch. The water from your roof is not immediately potable, of course, but your garden and houseplants will benefit from it. Many modern contraptions are closed systems, so you won't get leaves and other debris in the captured water and mosquitoes won't be able to get in and lay their eggs, bringing their irritating and potential disease-bearing presence into your back yard. If your system—like mine—is a little more loosey-goosey, there are products you can add to the water to kill the larvae. We add feeder goldfish to the water to do that work and feed them throughout the Fall, as the larvae are swallowed up.

It is so strange to most of us that there are homeowners associations with rules precluding water catchment and municipalities that have made nabbing rainwater illegal because the municipality claims to "own" it. This winds us back, as we always go, to the root of these matters. The root here is the vital importance and potential scarcity of potable water. So much of the Earth is wet, but much of that is saline and cannot be used to drink or water crops. We have invested so heavily in fossil fuels—oil, gas, and coal—with little consideration of the vital importance of water. Humans lived for many generations without the use of those fossil fuels, but we cannot survive at all without potable water. We have taken it—and the whole of the natural world on which our own species depends entirely—for granted, and we continue to do so at our peril. To spend an hour in the desert around a place like Las Vegas and then to enter the city is to experience a profound shock, a jarring of all the senses.

We can no more live without water than we can live without breathable air or nutritious food, but we scarcely give it a thought until it is threatened in some way, as we discussed in the essay on animism as a political and economic system.

Gutters and Having a Good Ladder

Gutters are engineering marvels that draw rainwater from the roof and into a water catchment barrel or other system. You can invest in special gutter caps that keep much of the falling debris out of the gutters, but they are an investment, to be sure. If you live in a one-story house and have made the very sensible investment in a good ladder, you can clean your own gutters. With these sorts of chores, it is always a good idea to have a helper to steady the ladder, hand you equipment, and get help if there's an accident. A helper makes the job more fun, too. We sometimes think we are "bothering" friends when we ask for this kind of assistance, but the truth is that everyone likes to feel they are needed and many hands really do make light work—or at least lighter work.

Pick a day after most of your trees have shed their leaves. You will need waterproof gloves, a trowel, and a lightweight bucket. Most of the gutter gunk can be scooped up by the handful and plopped into the bucket, but you may want the trowel for any bits that have already broken down. When your bucket is full, hand it down to your helper, and let her dump it onto the compost pile or into a larger container.

In many places, the first frost will arrive in the Samhain season, and that usually marks the end of gardening efforts. Still, there are some food crops that are made more delicious by the sharp blast of the first frost— Brussels sprouts are made sweeter by this exposure and there are several varieties of late apple that achieve their complete ripeness and maximum juice when the cold comes.

Apple Cider

These are the days to make apple cider, one of nature's special gifts to humanity. It is easily produced and a pleasure to drink and to give to friends, a bright ribbon wrapped around the bottle's neck. There are a couple of options for making cider—you can purchase ready-made apple juice, add some sugar and cider yeast, and ferment it with an airlock for several weeks. Then it's bottled and stored a bit longer. My preference is brown sugar for the yeast's food because it gives the cider a rich color and flavor. You can make a gallon or enough to fill a five-gallon glass bottle called a carboy.

If you are looking for a more complicated and satisfying process, you can start with apples, fresh from the orchard. Those apples require some cutting and mashing to create your gallons of juice. There are lots of tools to achieve juice—you can chop them up yourself and put them through a blender or food processor or you can buy or borrow a fruit press and mash those chopped apples to pulp, yielding fresh-pressed juice.

Whichever method you choose, cider is an ancient and nutritious drink, with enough of an alcohol kick to add a celebratory quality to any occasion, or no occasion at all. Make sure and label your bottles before you store them away. Consider giving your creation a fanciful name and printing some pretty labels on your home printer.

You can add other juices to the apple juice for something a little different. We've taken advantage of currants, blackberries, and raspberries in addition to apple for a colorful and delicious drink.

Apple Magic

I cannot let apple season pass without mentioning apple magic. Apples sliced horizontally reveal a star in their core and that sets up the road to magical consideration. In some cultures, it is considered good luck to peel an apple in one long strip. When that peel is thrown over the left shoulder, it creates an omen for the coming year and sometimes reveals the initial of someone who will become your paramour. Dried apples can be used as the face and head of special dolls, too.

Traditions and Celebrations

Death, Ghosts, and Origins of Hallowe'en

Hallowe'en is an American holiday that is based on older festivals that honor the dead. It has spread to many other countries with its peculiar combination of costumes, harvest games, and children going door to door, asking for treats. One of those older festivals is called Samhain, which is Gaeilge (Irish Gaelic) for "Summer's end." It harkens back, of course, to the era in western Europe when the year was divided into two parts—Summer and Winter.

It is a triple threat, this end of Summer. It is the end of the old agricultural year, the final harvest, and the festival of the dead. That's so much to consider in preparing for these days. Remember to slow down enough to enjoy the pleasures of this beautiful time.

Here is another holiday that I have borrowed from the Christian traditions—Martinmas. It called to me because of its association with the dead and with bonfires. It celebrates the end of the agrarian year, the harvest, and the completion of Winter preparations, including the butchering of animals. In some countries, Martinmas celebrations begin at the eleventh minute of the eleventh hour of this eleventh day of the eleventh month—that is, at 11:11 a.m. on November 11. In others, the festivities commence on St. Martin's Eve—that is, on November 10. Bonfires are built and children carry lanterns in the streets after dark, singing songs for which they are rewarded with candy.

Wild Foods: Foraging Opportunities in This Season

The land is yielding up its last harvest, too, and there are nuts, apples, and mushrooms to be gathered. Remember that the wild ones depend on these for the last fattening up and take only what you need.

Activities to Do with Children and Other Friends

So often seasonal activities are focused on children and families with children. But families are very different now—though they probably always were. There are plenty of couples who are childless, either intentionally or through the luck of the draw. Many of us have "chosen" families made up of friends so close we can't imagine our lives without them. Each of our seasons will contain a section on crafty, artsy activities that you can enjoy with children—yours or your chosen children-friends—with neighbors, or during a quiet afternoon at your own kitchen table.

In addition to creating or finding the perfect costume for the night of tricks and treats or a grown-up soiree, there are all sorts of delightful crafts to do with children and other friends in honor of this rich season. Nature's gifts are abundant—gourds, pumpkins, stooks of wheat, and shocks of corn. The gourds and pumpkins are a good place to begin, since they are an iconic part of the harvest season.

Both can be hollowed out and carved. If you are knife-shy, you can paint their thick skins with tempera paint or draw on them with markers. There are gourds that make birdhouses, and pumpkins have moved beyond the roundly segmented orange balls of yesteryear. They are so beautiful in their diversity that you may choose to grow and display many varieties—green and warty, white, miniature, or gigantic.

Costumes

We have moved so far from the creepy costumes of Depression-era America and even from the plastic mask-and-tunic-in-a-box from my childhood in the 1960s. If you are a person who enjoys designing clothes and likes to sew, this may be your best time. If you are not, there are always people who can help with that. Thrift stores are a good place to start for materials, as well as ideas.

As we consider the possibilities for Hallowe'en shenanigans, there is more on offer than simply escorting children on the neighborhood rounds. There are adult parties as well as rituals for the season, and it is good to keep in mind that costumes function as a portal to other states of consciousness and other ways of looking at the world.

Icon: Turnips

In Ireland and Scotland, the young, disguised beggars who wandered the lanes and roads in search of pennies and soul cakes carved root vegetables into lamps to light their way from house to house. Turnips were hollowed out, and holes shaped like mouths and eyes were carved on the front side, to let the burning tallow inside glow through. You can do the same thing at Samhaintide. Pick broad, untrimmed turnips for your lanterns. You want them untrimmed so that the tap root on the bottom forms a "beard" for your turnip-creature and resprouting leaves on the top make a proper hair-do. Slice the top of the turnip off and set it aside. Use a spoon to dig the pulpy flesh from the inside. This is surprisingly sweet and edible either raw or cooked. Make sure and leave a solid enough wall behind the purple and white skin—no need to dig out every drop of flesh. Dig the inside base of the turnip so it's as flat as possible—a small candle will set there. Use a soft pencil to draw eyes, nose, and mouth on the skin and then carve them out with a sharp paring knife.

Season's End

Like each of our markers in the agricultural year, Samhain holds opportunities for a renewal of our spiritual values by participating in the turning of the Wheel. This participation anchors us into the land whereon we bide so that the roots we grow are regenerative for ourselves and the land. As we anticipate six weeks of long nights, each a little longer than the one before, we can give ourselves the gift of watching the dark skies and feeling our smallness when compared to the arc of the star-filled space above us. Healing flows out on the cooling winds, and as the leaves fade and drop to the earth, we can start to claim the oneness that has for so long eluded us.

2

The Solstice of Winter:
A Thoughtful Quarter Day

Hush now. All the world awaits.
Ghosts arise, pale songs sung late.
Solstice morning, rise and shine,
The light renews itself so fine.
The dark night shrinks as day grows long
And ghosts retreat with whispered song.

Letter from the Forest-Farm: In the Midwinter Woods

OH, TO BE IN A FOREST IN WINTER! There is no better place to experience the most perfect of silences. A fulsome snow gives us a chance to play ancient tracker and guess the footprints' owners, wondering where their journeys are taking them. The trees are naked and stand tall, revealing every branch and twig. Dark against the grey sky, the leaves of Summer trampled wetly beneath the heavy snow, they know different things than we do. Their lives are longer than ours, their power of observation keener because their circle of effect is smaller than ours. Trees practice slow-seeing and always have. We are learning more about the layer of mycelium that covers much of the planet but are only now touching on its importance and the dizzying variety of fungi it contains. Trees may communicate through it, and it may also hold the key to communication between here and the Otherworlds we pondered in the first part of this book.

The stark silhouettes, bereft of leaf and blossom, are not the only trees in the wood. The abundance of deciduous trees sometimes masks the others in the forest, the constant ones that are evergreen. Our eyes catch that brightness against the grey and white picture of the land in Winter. It is hard to resist touching their needles, and I rarely do, brushing a droopy branch and then lifting my fingers to my nose to take in the evocative fragrance.

During the six weeks following the feast of the dead at Samhain, there is a sense of expectation centered on longer days, our superstitious fear of darkness soothed for a time. These long nights offer us many opportunities for renewal and rest, things that our spirits need as surely as our bodies do. Like the summertime skinks who regrow their tails or the starfish that regrow lost arms, we can plan and work for a kind of regeneration of our physical and ethereal selves. Give yourself—as well as the people who depend on you—the gift of a rested you who is thinking more clearly and able to adjust to a depth of feeling that your exhausted self simply couldn't manage.

This Embertide: Seed-Hold

This Ember Day is the first in our agricultural calendar. It occurs within the aura of the Winter Solstice, the time when the daylight begins to lengthen as the night subsides, signaling the renewal of the agricultural cycle. As we reinvent Ember Days, we will find the way into a spiritual broadening and deepening of each Embertide, tying it into the season in which it resides. At the little farm, we approach this Embertide in a practical way: we are drying the saved seed from the most recent growing season and preserving it for the upcoming planting. Different seeds require different preservation techniques. The easiest are the self-seeding plants, which are often annuals but sometimes biennial. These require nothing at all from the grower, except maybe not to weed them out of the bed because you forgot they were there. The second easiest are beans and peas, which I leave at the end of the season as I let the hulls dry on the vine as the Winter weather kills the vines that hold them. Sometime in this time leading up to the Solstice, I'll pull the dry hulls off, and clean them at the kitchen table, releasing the dried beans and peas. These can be used as dried beans and reconstituted by cooking in plenty of water. But most will be stored in airtight containers to be next year's beans.

Since we are using these Embertides for spiritual reflection and renewal, let's tie in ideas of seed-saving and find out what it tells us about our beliefs and our worldview. First, we remove the hulls and let them fall away, as the leaves fell from the branches. When we shed the leaves of stale practice and unlearn some of the things we have carried from our earliest days on these paths—the things that weren't true, the things that didn't fit—we stand like the trees in their naked power. Consider what you are called to unlearn so that you can make space for the wisdom the earth and your Ancestors have to teach you. We can do more than simply follow the seasons—though to do that brings a great deal of satisfaction and, to be honest, is often done in the most cursory way.

By clearing away the clutter of those inaccurate beginner books and your early training with teachers who cared more for their public presentation than for their students, you are able to make some different decisions about what you need to know and, indeed, who you really are.

Skills

Storytelling Part II: Mythmaking

At the deepest heart of every human is a need for the instruction and the release of story. The tales that come down to us through our cultural and combined histories are books we return to again and again to find guidance during times of stress, of joy, of fear.

In the previous chapter we looked at the homely stories of family myth—the lessons that define us for either good or ill. As we sit by our Winter fire, with the family legends dangling like trophies from our belts, it is time to widen the net of these learnings and reach for the universal qualities that release our humanity into a larger realm.

One of my favorite media is the guided meditation, strolling into the places beyond the time and space over which we feel we have some ownership and into a region of mist, improbable journey, and those monsters that haunt both our inner and outer human landscape. Now that the stories of our personal Ancestors have been committed once again to our collective memory, we turn onto the pathway over the great forest and into the worlds of imagination and remembered wonder.

We can always begin with the stories we call "fairy tales": there is a quest laid down and then a journey, some complications, meetings both fair and foul, hardships overcome, and a resolution at the last. It is a satisfying order straight from the pages of Aristotle's *Poetics*. But these tales of long ago and far away don't belong to us in the sense of our family tales. These are other people, far away. How can their experiences—no matter how adventurous—tell us how to be in the modern world, where we have sucked the soul from the material world around us? And you know the answer, after all. When we re-enchant the world around us, we make this mythic journey, this learning and instruction, immediate again. And when we dig those deep furrows into what plagues us now as systems fail all around us, we come back again and again to the natural world and our renewed and re-valued presence in the workings of it.

Charles Dickens knew the value of this old/new telling of tales, and we encounter one of his most accessible works at the Winter Solstice most years. *A Christmas Carol* has all that we need to satisfy this journey. The characters are recognizable even today—the mean and unyielding boss, the wage slave, the very rich, and the very poor. There are children and elders and everyone in between. Food is important, even in its scarcity.

When Scrooge chooses thin gruel as his supper, even though he could have roasted meat and cake, we know something about his brokenness as well as his disconnection with self, with family, with nature itself.

And there are ghosts—because whether we acknowledge them or not, there are always ghosts. Dickens's ghosts are personal, agenda-driven, and unignorable, as our personal ghosts tend to be. Sit by your fire and tell the stories of the mythic past as you create the mythic present and build the foundations for the potential of a mythic future, rooted in good earth and our personal experiences as an integral part of the natural world.

Firewood

Before Enlightenment, chop wood, carry water. After Enlightenment, chop wood, carry water.

—Zen proverb

Many of us no longer live lives where water must be carried and firewood chopped—more's the pity. Chopping firewood is excellent exercise and works many important muscle groups. In addition, it provides instant gratification. You swing and chop, then make a tidy stack that will feed your fireplace, woodstove, or firepit. The stack grows steadily, and you will be rewarded with warmth on cold days and a bright fire to cheer you.

Fiberwork

As the nights creep in upon us, there is a warmth to handling roving and yarn and a satisfaction in creating warm garments to pass along to others or to wear yourself. Roving is wool and other fibers that have been cleaned by washing and then carded. It is often already dyed and ready to be spun into yarn. Yarn comes in a variety of colors, fibers, and thicknesses, and each of them has particular uses.

Roving becomes yarn through the act of spinning, and it is best to begin here. And we start by looking at the folkloric and mythic place of this transformative art. From the spinners of the ancient world Ariadne and Arachne to the unnamed miller's daughter in the story of Rumpelstiltskin to the recent renewed interest in fleece-to-value-added product, the transformation of plant-based and animal-sourced fibers is filled with practical magic. It has also long been considered women's work, though that is somewhat less likely now.

Silkworms and spiders give us the exquisite material of silk, and a product more evocative is hard to imagine. It also harkens back to our reconnections into the natural world and through the landscape of both myth and history. Any culture with spiders has tales of these divine creatures, and science assures us that the spider's silk is extraordinarily strong. There are spider divinities—Spider Grandmother and the trickster Anansi are two—who remind us of the web of all being, which is strong when tended and acknowledged but can be weakened and even broken if left unattended and neglected. There are also divine beings that spin the fate of individual humans, and they are usually found in threes—the third holding shears or a knife with which to cut the thread when the life cycle of that particular person is at an end.

Distaff and Women's Work

A few words must be said about these arts. For many years, they were the province of women. The word *distaff* has come to mean the female and the mother side of one's family, but a distaff is a spindle upon which the spun fiber is wound before it is used in weaving. That it is also a magical tool—as is the spindle—can hardly be surprising. In some northern European cultures, this women's implement was thought to be the thing that witches rode to their rendezvous, once again coupling women's tools with the potentially malicious work of witches.

Drop Spindles and Spinning Wheels

Drop spindles are tricky things, and it is easy to imagine that they are the piskies of older lore. They are simple tools, easily made by hand, as well as available from craft and yarn stores. A spindle usually is a long rod about a foot long with a hook on the bottom. It is topped with a flat, rounded disc through which the rod protrudes. There are other styles, too, and they tend to differ according to the culture of origin. A spindle spins roving into thread or yarn and does so through the act of spinning. My journey to this mesmerizing art began a decade ago when our women's group met to share wine and craft projects. One of the women had a drop spindle and promised to teach me. But I ended up learning from a YouTube video and have continued to this day. I acquire roving as I can and spin when I am able and have time for this gentle and important art. It is especially sweet to use the wool from sheep I know or to purchase it from women who raise animals for fiber.

Spinning wheels are a much more recent creation and yet they loom large in our imaginations. These tools are incredibly intuitive—to coordinate the spin and the tension of the feed—and spinning is meditative to both perform and observe. There are standing wheels as well as wheels that are foot-operated by a seated spinner.

Any of these tools is designed to create yarn, and there are many other tools and techniques for working yarn or thread into an entirely different form. We will travel now down this woolly road—from sheep to shearer, from washing to combing, from carding to roving, from spinning to the next steps.

For our purposes, we will look at embroidery, weaving, knitting, felting, and crochet. This will be a brief introduction on each of these as there are many books on each subject as well as educational videos and local classes and artisans that can teach you these fine and practical arts. All of them can be practiced with relatively conservative outlays of money—with the possible exception of weaving.

Embroidery

Embroidery and other thread decorations are also making a comeback, and that is a very good thing. This is another simple and beautiful art that can be done by the youngest beginner and perfected through the years. As with most fiber projects, these are meditative as well as practical.

Knitting

Knitting can be as simple or as elaborate as you choose to engage with it. The tools are simple enough and include needles—which come in several styles including double-ended and circular—gauges, and yarn. I taught myself to knit when my daughter was eight years old, and her favorite teacher was an enthusiastic knitter. My daughter never took to it, but the rhythm of the process enchanted me and I have been knitting ever since. I am, however, the least ambitious of knitters and confine myself to scarves, shawls, and wash cloths. I often find myself in long meetings from which I derive little or no satisfaction or even information. When I bring my knitting with me, the action keeps me relaxed but alert, and at the end of the meeting, I will often have a finished scarf. That scarf can become a gift for someone I care for, or I can donate it to my local homeless people's support group or women's shelter. Most of my yarn comes from sales at craft stores, from thrift shopping, and from friends who have gotten bored with knitting and want to clear room in their craft closet for a new endeavor.

Felting and Needle Felting

Stabbing with tiny needles—what could be more satisfying? Felting is the act of binding together wool, matting it into a sheet that can be used for other projects, like warm collars and cuffs. Wet felting is done by washing a knitted piece like a sweater or scarf and pounding it with a wooden tool that is shaped like a small iron and causes the fibers to mat up. It can also be accomplished through a process called needle felting. The tools you need for that are almost as simple as your knitting tools. You'll need a block of heavy foam, special felting needles, a needle holder, and hanks of roving in colors that please you. Laying the roving across the block of foam, you stab it until the fibers mesh together. This technique is often used to make dolls, purses, and decorations. The needles are very sharp—be careful in your exuberant stabbing. The results have a softly ethereal quality, and the final product is warm and water resistant.

Crochet

There's a bit of a competition between some knitters and crocheters. The techniques are different and the tools diverge, but the creation of clothing and accessories by the use of a simple tool in the hands of an experienced practitioner has the same satisfaction and level of artistic achievement whichever tool and technique are employed. The tools needed for crochet are as easily acquired as the ones for knitting: crochet hooks, stitch markers, a measuring tape, and yarn.

Weaving

This activity is neither simple nor inexpensive, but the satisfaction and the beauty of creation more than make up for it. Many of us had small looms as children, looms that helped us create beaded panels for jewelry and those funny square looms with upright prongs on which we wove innumerable potholders with little loops on the corner.

Fabric looms come in several sizes and can be purchased disassembled. From the smaller ones that create woven pendants and textured wall hangings to the enormous commercial looms that create yardage, and everything in between, weaving is an intense meditation when done by a weaver sitting at her bench, bent on the act of creation. The setup for weaving takes some time and concentration: the warp is lined up first and these threads run forward and back along the length of the loom. The weaving happens when the weft—the thread that runs crosswise on the loom—is pushed through the warp with a shuttle and then pressed into the rows preceding it with a comb. Then the weft is woven through again from the other side and this process continues until the piece is complete.

Throughout history, weaving appears in the stories of our Ancestors both as women's work and as acts of piety by the weavers. Tapestries graced royal halls and functioned as visual aids for the stories of the house and family. These tapestries were often woven by the women of the house, nobly born and nobly bored. Weavers created sacred garments for the enormous statues of the gods that graced antiquity. Penelope wove to dissuade her suitors in the *Odyssey* as she awaited her husband's prolonged return from the Trojan War. Weaving holds promise as well as history, and like so many of the things we're exploring, it ties us into the webs of history and the cycles that maintain and inform us.

Chores

Draft Dodgers

Some of you will remember when the Selective Service drafted able-bodied young men into the US armed forces. Young men must still register with the Selective Service when they turn eighteen. If they fail to do so, they used to be called draft dodgers. That is not the sort of draft dodger we're talking about here, though. If you live in an older house, mobile home, or apartment, there may be significant gaps at the bottom of the doors leading outside. You can reset the door, if you have the skills, or you can have the door reset by someone who does. This is not always possible with older doors and door frames, so you may choose to make and deploy a draft dodger. These are fat snakes made of fabric stuffed with batting, popcorn, or cat litter. Make them for drafty windows, too.

Cleaning and Sharpening Tools

At the end of the gardening season—not that it ever really ends—it is wise to spend a little time cleaning your tools, both large and small. As with any tool, it is best to clean as you go, but sometimes the work gets the better of us and we get to the end of the season with soil still clinging to the shaft of our shovel and a dull edge on our hoe. Take the time before Winter gets too far in to clean all the debris off, sharpen anything that needs it, and lightly oil the metal parts. A sturdy bucket full of coarse sand is a good choice for the initial cleaning. Get some plain steel wool at the hardware store for the next part and remember to wear work gloves when you use it: steel wool has a very bad habit of leaving little splinters in uncovered fingers. If you really have knocked a nick in your favorite hoe, you may need to grind the edge with a hand grinder or sandpaper to get it useful again. Before you stack them all in your tool shed—or porch or back room—give them a little smear of oil—WD-40 will do nicely—and thank them for their help throughout the season. I sing mine a lullaby, but you may not choose to go quite that far. Don't forget to clean your hand tools, too, and dump the detritus out of your tools bag or basket.

Sewing

As you leave the outdoor world to its season of dormancy and rest, it's a good time to think about sewing up some warm garments for the coming months or to dream of Summer and plot what you will do with that bright and flowing cotton you found on sale at your local fabric store. There are many ways to sew and several tools to do it. You can sew by hand or with a machine, and there are options there, too. There are heavy machines in cabinets, portable machines of varying sizes, and non-electric treadle machines, both antique and modern.

Hand-sewing is the cheapest way, but it takes more time. It requires a packet of needles in varying sizes and sewing thread in black and white and a few colors. It is wise to practice making small stitches as they will secure the pieces of fabric better and the result will last longer. Hand-sewing is also used for projects like quilting and hemming, though those can also be done by machine. It is imperative that you learn to make a good strong knot at the beginning of a row of stitching and to execute another one when you finish a place. These knots secure your stitches and keep the pieces together.

Electric Machine—Table or Portable

Most people who sew use an electric machine for all the reasons listed above. Some have machines in built-in cabinets that are opened up to use. Most, however, use portable sewing machines that are tucked away in a specially fitted case and brought out only for projects.

Treadle Machine

This is a machine that is operated by foot, pushing a flat treadle up and down. A belt connects the treadle to a wheel on the side of the machine to move the needle up and down. These are often antiques, but new ones can be found in Amish country. They are modern machines attached to a treadle case.

Patterns

Sewing clothing is easiest when you use a paper pattern. These come in every size and can be adjusted by carefully measuring the body of the person who will wear the garment and comparing it to the paper pattern. A fabric store will have fat pattern books that can be pored over to create all sorts of garments, as well as household items like pillows and covers for small kitchen appliances. You won't need a pattern for plain curtains, napkins, or tablecloths—these only require careful cutting and hemming.

Traditions and Celebrations

The Yuletide and Giving Thanks

Greenery

Bringing in the Greens has been an important part of Midwinter cele-brations in many parts of the Northern Hemisphere. The symbolism is important, of course—that even in this time of short days, a brightening of the heart can be achieved by cutting evergreen boughs and carrying their scent and color and life into the hearth, the home. There are plenty of places in most communities to purchase either a cut tree or one with attached root ball, as well as garlands and wreathes of evergreens. You may live near an area where these trees are grown, and you can go through the rows and choose the one that best fits the room in which it will be housed. Then you can cut it or the farmer will do that for you, bag it for travel, and help you to tie it onto your car.

In our best of all possible worlds, where a little forest-farm is the place where you abide, you may choose to plant a hedge of fast-growing pine from which you choose the perfect specimen each year, planting a replacement for every one you take. You may also choose to get a serviceable artificial tree from your favorite thrift store and use it year after year, only bringing into your home the pruned branches at the edge of the wood.

Whichever way you choose to honor the season, this is the time when nature gives us a time for rest and reflection, as we noted in our earlier discussion of the Wheel of the Year. Let us consider stepping back from the capitalist madness of the Winter holiday season and remember the plain joys of being together at the hearth, giving gifts from the heart and hand, and finding the intense pleasure of true rest. If that sounds nothing at all like the rush of your holiday seasons but immeasurably better, you might want to try it.

Gifts

We will look at some crafty possibilities for gifts in a little while, but first let us consider the idea of giving and how it can bind us and remind us of our intentional kinship with the biosphere. If the thought of gifts gives you the grippe, it would be wise to consider why you choose to do so in the first place. If it is a cultural or familial obligation, you may be able to articulate to yourself and others why you find it difficult or objectionable.

You may have too many people you feel you must give to and the number is overwhelming. It could be a financial burden at a time when property taxes and other pulls on your resources are difficult to balance. There may always be a formal gift for your boss or a distant and unknown relative that will always be an obligation of the season, and if that is the case, you can choose to think of it as your sacrifice to the common peace in either workplace or extended family and leave it at that. You can choose to be the quirky gift giver who gives every single person on their list the same gift, whether it is bright yellow socks to mimic the "return" of the Sun or a jar of orange marmalade for the same reason. The point is you decide how you will engage with the overriding cultural miasma of seasonal gift-giving that affects even those who don't celebrate any particular holiday at this time. You like the idea of the yellow socks though, don't you?

Welcoming the Holy Child

In cultures where the Winter Solstice is acknowledged through ceremony and celebration, myths have grown up around the Divine Child and its birth in this time of renewal. We have Baby New Year, as well as the various divine figures whose births are placed at the time of the Winter Solstice. Whether you choose to welcome a Child, symbolic or mythic, at this time may depend on the culture you claim or in which you dwell. The idea is so sweet and filled with promise it is well worth the celebration, whatever shape you choose to give to it.

Sitting Vigil

There are many opportunities throughout the year to commemorate an event or the anniversary of an event through a vigil. We will look at two different kinds of vigils here and consider how best to prepare for each one in ways that make it meaningful as well as powerful. Short vigils are a help to draw attention to an occurrence that has profoundly moved a particular community or group, and organizers have determined that a gathering in a public place, often with special speakers, with prayer and community song, is called for. Acts of violence seem to call out for these gatherings, which sometimes take place in the evening when the largest number of people are free from work or school obligations and can choose to participate. Sometimes a brief and solemn walk is part of such a vigil as people gather in one place and process to the location of the vigil. These often include candles, and there is something particularly beautiful about a line of people, their faces lit by their soft light, walking in procession to a place of reckoning. It brings up some of our oldest cultural memories, many clothed in religious trappings, and sets an appropriate mood for the continuing proceedings.

Another sort of vigil is a sort of endurance trial of expectation and can be experienced singly or in a group. I mention it here because sitting up all night awaiting the dawn is an experience that everyone should try to have at least once in their lives. Winter Solstice is a perfect time for such a vigil as we welcome the renewed Sun in its rising following the longest night of the year. It is a promise that comes down to us through our DNA from our earliest Ancestors, and the re-enactment is intensely satisfying. I suggest you gather a group of like-minded folks, stack enough wood for a night of campfire, and have everyone bring food and drink to share. Depending on your climate, you will need to dress accordingly and may even bring sleeping bags and blankets. You may choose to remain awake the entire night—that is the endurance trial part—or you may take it in shifts to have a short nap, as long as there are wakeful people who are tending the fire and watching out for each other as the night season snuggles in. There will be stories and song, merriment and grief, for that is the way of fire and long nights when friends gather to bring in the new year.

Wild Foods: Foraging Opportunities in This Season

There are few foraging opportunities in this season. Most of the wild foods have, quite rightly, gone into the bellies of our wild kindred, and we have stored provisions for these lean times. This is a good time to repair your gathering baskets, learn new wild foods, and let the land continue its sleep.

Activities to Do with Children and Other Friends

Bird and Bat Houses

Making little houses is a favorite activity for lots of children. The youngest are happy with a cardboard cylinder that used to hold oatmeal and can be adapted with paint and glued treasures and a door cut out and windows drawn on into a truly tiny house. The next step up from that is bird and bat houses. There are kits for creating them, but the plans are easily cobbled together with the help of an adult who can use a saw, some scrap wood, paint, and ingenuity. Neither birds nor bats are nesting at this time of year, so you have plenty of time to figure it out, cut it out, put it together, and paint it before it is really needed. Birdhouses are shaped differently from bat houses, and the designs are available in magazines and online.

Knitting

As we noted in the previous chapter, knitting is easy and it is an activity that helps with hand to eye coordination for children, folks with disabilities, and even elders who are living with cognitive issues. It helps focus attention and requires minimal skill, a couple of knitting needles, and some yarn. Knitting needles come in many sizes, but for this activity I recommend some big fat needles and thick yarn. The size of both will work best for little fingers, arthritic fingers, and new-to-the-task fingers. The other advantage is that knitting a scarf with these materials is quick work, with near-instant gratification. You can make your own knitting needles, which make sweet gifts for friends with are newly enamored with knitting. Pick up a thick dowel at the craft or hardware store and find beads with big holes that will slip onto the end of the dowel and then get glued into place. A sharp pocketknife will give you a good but not too sharp point at the other end of the needle and a careful pass over the whole needle with some sandpaper will make it smooth and easy to handle. Scarves for everyone!

Peanut Butter and Seed Pine Bird Feeders

Easily one of the messiest projects you will do with your friends, both large and small, this requires pine cones, peanut butter, bird seed, recycled containers to hold the finished product, and some twine. Cut a twelve-inch length of twine, double it, and thread it through the top part of the pine cone, then tie it in a knot. It is important that you do this part first because it will be too sticky to do that later. Hold it up and wiggle it to make sure the twine is threaded through enough to keep the pine cone in the loop. Pour bird seed onto some newspaper or into a low dish on the table. Smear the pine cone with peanut butter using a light touch—if the peanut butter is in heavy globs it is likely to fall off once you've dipped the cone in the seed. That's the next step—roll the pine cone in the seed and mash the seed into the peanut butter with your finger. Tuck the bird feeder into a container and take it outside to a tree limb, making sure you can observe it from a window in the house if you'd like to see which birds accept your invitation.

Icons: Wreaths

Simply put, wreaths are circles of greenery that adorn a door or gate. Their significance at this time of year harkens back to the fresh and living green that draws us out of the Midwinter and propels us forward to the hope and promise of Spring. The circle reminds us of our dear Wheel of the Year and the agricultural cycle that ties us to the rest of our Earth kindred. A circle is also a wheel that moves us through the cycles of our lives as well as those of nature.

Greenery is something that can be gathered from your land, of course, but there is a brisk business at this time of year in cut greens—including trees. Check with friends, neighbors, and the tree stand in the ice cream shop's parking lot to see if you can have the branches that were trimmed from the home-bound trees.

Wreaths can be in any sort of material. We make sturdy ones from the trimmed grapevines at the end of that harvest. These can be left plain or decorated with all sorts of natural objects like pine cones and sweet gum balls and also with pretty ribbon and golden ornaments.

The intention of placing a circular wreath on the entryway to your living space reminds you, with every entrance and exit, that the year moves forward, the times change. If your personal life has been especially challenging through this darkening time, the wreath is a symbol of all that is possible with the Solstice. That includes healing for you and a culmination of those challenges into a course of action that moves your life in a different and more satisfying direction.

Season's End

We won't observe the profound change that happens at this Solstice when the darkness begins its retreat. It will take several weeks before most people can tell that the bright section of the day is lengthening. You may, however, feel a difference, especially in the people around you. Instead of engaging these last weeks of rest, we have been racked by the challenges of family and of the culture. With these pressures off, we look towards the cultural New Year celebration on January I with a sense of anticipation of joy and delight. Consider, though, the six weeks before our next marker—Imbolc and Candlemas—and know that this midwinter time holds mystery and some danger. Keep your wits about you and try to capture some of the renewal you missed from Samhain until the Winter Solstice.

3

The Season of Imbolc:
Light in Hand, in Heart, in Hearth

Snow on crocus, ice on spring,
Imbolc's heart holds everything.
Still in darkest morning go
Gather chickweed's greenly show.
Early signs of vernal thaw
Healing, poetry, smithcraft all!

Letter from the Forest-Farm: Seated in the Season of Ice and Mud

THERE IS A DENTED TIN BOX ON MY DESK that is filled with holey stones, which I have collected for many years. A true holey stone (sometimes called a hag stone or Odin's eye) is a small stone that has a naturally occurring hole in it. The hole must go right through the stone so that you can hold it up to your eye and see through it. They are used for many things magically, including easy childbirth and scrying. They usually come from stone beaches—as opposed to sandy ones—where the constant action of the water works on imperfections in the rock and wears a hole in it over a long period of time.

I mention this because the little forest-farm seems to shake off the Winter doldrums at Imbolc as surely as the water wears a hole in rock.

The early signs are subtle—a spot of green in a sheltered place, the emergence of snow drops' folded leaves tucked against the rock wall. As our eyes adjust, we notice markers everywhere. The air smells different. It isn't warm by any means, but it feels more malleable somehow, less perpetual, as though a break in its waves could let in more warmth—not now but later: a promise of Beltane and harvest as seen upside-down through an old-fashioned gazing ball.

This season is often dedicated to the pan-Celtic goddess Brigid, who is known as both smith and midwife, as well as a score of other very practical things. The soil does its expanding and contracting dance with every thaw-and-freeze sequence of late Winter.

The woods still keep their secrets though. The neighborhood hawk drops a morsel of rabbit near the mugwort bed, and the groundhog has once again found an entryway into the earthen basement in the little farmhouse. We can hear her down there settling in, no doubt getting her den ready for some adorable and destructive babies to arrive in the coming weeks. There are no leaves unfurling yet, but some tight nubs that will become buds have appeared on the tips of three of the young apple trees. The fourth looks sparse and wasted and may not have survived the Winter. It will stay amongst its siblings for now, in hopes that it is literally a late bloomer.

There is some rain now. Cold and sloppy, the soil drinks in what it can and the rest runs into gullies and low-lying places in the land. The leaves from last Fall still lie on the yard in front of the house and the planting beds in the back, delivering the last of their nutrients to the thin soil of this region. Much of their bulk will completely break down in the Spring rains next month, and we'll only have to rake them out of the corners and edges of walls and from underneath the clothes line.

People come from all sorts of places to visit these mountains when the "colors" are at their peak in October. Many homeowners, however, can't wait to rake up the mess, as they see it. We like to watch the subtle and beautiful transition here at the farm. The gold and red carpets begin to lose their magnificent color almost as soon as they leave the mother trees. They brown in the weak light of November and are buffeted by all that Winter offers here. When I brush them away from the pea fence, as I did today, they still have such a soft beauty about them. The oak leaves are still glossy and leathery, but the maples and poplars have little left of their original shape, the ragged remnants clinging to the stick that used to be the leaf's supple spine.

Humans are much the same. We stick to our function in the young days, green and shading. But the clinging can't last and the life force, like the tree's chlorophyll, begins to ebb a bit. We find other gifts and other ways of being useful—tending children, dispensing any wisdom we may have accumulated in our years. We are a covering for those in our charge, the way fallen leaves cover and protect the plants below them through the weather of Winter. At the very last, our lives and legacies are left to the winds of new days and we fade, coming to rest on the land of the Ancestors, as last Fall's leaves come to reside on the compost heap, there to become new soil.

Skills

Broom-Making

We will make much of the homely broom in this season of change. Most of us purchase brooms at the hardware store, but they can also be fun to make. You can choose to grow a patch of broom corn and dry it for use as the head of your broom. Or you can buy a bundle of broom or broom corn online if that fits your lifestyle best. Finding the handle will be the challenging part, especially for those of you who are urban-dwellers. I recommend starting with a short broom, like a whisk broom or crumb broom. Find a stout stick, about six inches long.

You'll need your bundle of broom straw, some heavy twine or lightweight wire—eight gauge should work—and the strong stick you discovered in the park. With a penknife, carefully strip the bark from your stick. Determine how long the head will be. A crumber can have fairly short straws, but a whisk broom likes a longer head. Tie little bundles of the broom straw and bind them together with the twine or wire. These bundles should be about as big around as a pencil, and you will need at least a dozen of them. Tie them up tightly but not so tightly that you break the straw. When they are all assembled, bind them one by one to the stick, balancing them all around its circumference. Give it the finishing touch of binding the whole shebang together with the wire or twine. You can use a piece of colorful hemp twine to finish off your creation's binding. Take some kitchen shears and give the little broom a haircut to level off the bottom of the brush.

Firecraft: Striking New Fire

This particular skill is important and there are plenty of tools to help you perfect it as well as techniques to achieve the desired effect. Here are a few of those techniques. All of these methods require tiny pieces of dry tinder (leaves, paper), fluff of some sort that will quickly ignite (milkweed, thistle, cattail), and your breath.

Fire Bow/Friction Method

This is a more practical way to rub two sticks together and make a fire through the heat of friction. A tool that is shaped like an archery bow (but much smaller) is used to drill into a piece of wood into which a shallow indentation has been scraped.

Fire Striker/Flint Method

By striking a piece of flint or another stone that sparks against a second stone, you can concentrate the sparks onto small dry tinder. When it begins to smoke, blow on it gently until a small flame is established.

Burning Glass/Solar Method

We've seen it in cartoons—someone holds a big magnifying glass and directs the Sun's energy to set something on fire. It happens instantaneously—the object bursts into flames. The principle is the same with this solar method, but the time frame is not accurate.

Chores

Averting Frost Damage

Depending on where you live, the weather—temperature, precipitation, and wind—will invite you to fall in love with these perfect days and to have your heart broken by the fickleness of it all. The chance of late cold snaps or frosts is a real danger in the garden, so have your wits about you when the temperature threatens to fall below acceptable levels. You can cover tender plants with old bed sheets, plastic milk jugs with the flat bottom cut out, or a thin fabric or plastic to act as a row cover. Decide which works best for your purposes and have them on hand.

Mushrooms and Mushrooms Logs

It is unlikely that there are mushrooms to forage at this time, but it's a lovely time to make inoculated logs from which mushrooms will spring in a few months. Many garden centers offer how-to classes, and you can even take home a log to water and keep warm. We have two in a long pail in the kitchen, and we peer at them in hopes of seeing some delicious fungus.

Stringing Pea Fences and Prepping the Pea Trellis

Peas and brassicas (cabbage, broccoli, cauliflower) are the earliest things you can plant in most areas, if you don't have a poly-tunnel or row cover. Your work last Fall in putting the garden to bed including a layer of composted manure has now worked its magic on the soil below. The bed is ready for peas to be pushed into the soil, and the supports for them are best put into place when they are planted. I always tell myself that I'll do that trellis later—there's plenty of time. But there isn't plenty of time, and the four-inch-high pea plants wobble around until I get to putting up the strings for them to climb. Do it with the planting—or even before. Your peas will thank you, and you'll be pleased that you didn't procrastinate.

Here at the little farm, we put spinach seeds in the ground in the Fall, but now is the second best time. Pick a day that is warmish and fair and put a row in the garden. Sow lavishly—you will be able to thin-and-eat before you know it.

Indoors: Take advantage of a sunny window. South-facing is the best. Use a plastic tub about four inches deep, and fill it with soil or planting medium—which is soil with some additions. Start some baby greens—lettuces, spinach, arugula, bok choi—and watch them peek up and start to grow. Be vigilant about watering these babies and make sure they have good, bright light.

Traditions and Celebrations

In addition to the joys of Imbolc, this season boasts the very celebration of Love Itself, Valentine's Day. Like most things in our modern culture, there is controversy about the origins of this popular tradition—who was St. Valentine and isn't this all based on some sort of Pagan Roman thing? You may certainly do all the research you want on this subject and come down on whatever side best pleases you. But to honor the romantic (and otherwise!) notions of bonding amongst our human community is something to be considered.

Make remembrances for friends and family—simple cutouts of hearts are often perfect. Or use your expertise in the complicated business of collage creation to craft works of heart and art for those same beloveds. Mail them! Hand deliver them! But don't buy those awful packages from the drugstore with the latest Disney characters on them—unless that is just the thing that will show your beloveds how you feel. Hugs and kisses are also a welcome addition.

At the farm, we will use anything as an excuse to break into song and scamper around in an awkward but enthusiastic dance. Clear out the Winter dust from your throat with a good cup of tea and sing a song to the sky and the still-cold earth and to your companions on the journey through this Wheel of the Year. Sing loudly—if badly—and rejoice in the bellows that are your lungs and the vocal cords that go their ways to make sound possible.

You might even try singing for a mate, as the birds are doing outside the window right now. Righteously. Insistently. Ferociously.

Wild Foods: Foraging Opportunities in This Season

There are not too many foraging opportunities in these early days but as you walk on the land you may be lucky to find early stinging nettles and the sweet greenness of chickweed. There may also be a little dandelion action—eat them up! Remember, stinging nettle tea is full of good nutrition, and nettle is also good as pesto sauce.

Activities to Do with Children and Other Friends

This season of Brigid is full of frolicsome things to do with children. In the spirit of Father Christmas, Brigid travels around the world, accompanied by her little cow. She blesses the households along her path, and householders leave some grain for the cow and a drink for Brigid. Sometimes Brigid leaves little gifts for the children in the family, and that is certainly something you can adopt for your little ones. And because Brigid has so far to travel, the children can make a little bed for her to rest upon. We always made ours from a cardboard shoe box, filled with cotton batting. We tucked a cloth napkin firmly around the mattress and added a tiny pillow made from cotton squares covered in toilet tissue. Another pretty cloth napkin makes a blanket. Leave it near a fireplace or hearth, if you have one. If not, leave it on a central table, along with the bowl of grain and the little glass of drink.

The young ones can also be cajoled into blessing the house, in Brigid's name. If the weather permits, have them stage themselves in front of the front door. Their role is to knock loudly while the adults wait inside, preferably with soda bread and hot chocolate for these little players. Knock. From inside: "Who is it?" Children: "It's Brigid!" No answer. The second round of knocking is a little louder, especially if they know there's hot chocolate waiting for them. Knock! Knock! Knock! Again, from inside: "Who is it?" Children: "It's Brigid!" No answer. The last set of knocks are set to shake the house. KNOCK! KNOCK! KNOCK! Giggling adults respond: "Who is it?" Children: "It is Brigid! We've come to bless the house!"

The door is opened, and the children are welcomed in with much fanfare. They walk into and out of each room, bestowing blessings while keeping one eye on the treats that are waiting for them. The children are in on the whole thing, so you aren't being mean—only building suspense.

Candle-Making

The goddess Brigid, as well as her saintly twin, is a fire goddess and has an eternal sacred flame in her hometown of Kildare in Ireland. Since Imbolc is often thought of as her holiday, making pretty candles to use or to give away makes good sense.

The easiest way to do this is by using beeswax sheets. These can be ordered online, but please check your local craft and art supply store to see if they carry them and encourage them to, if they don't. You'll also need some lengths of wicking, and it is worth it to spend a little extra to get non-toxic wicking that doesn't emit nastiness when burned. Before you begin the project, move the wax to the warmest room in your house—my choice is always my kitchen. Cut a length of wick one inch longer than the length of the wax sheet and place it at one end of the sheet. Fold the end over the wick and mash it into place with your fingers. Do this slowly so that the heat of your fingers softens the wax as you go. When the entire wick—except for the one-inch excess—is embedded in the wax, you may start to carefully roll the sheet into a tube. For the very best results when burning the candle, roll it firmly but not too tight. There is one final touch that will hold your creation together—seal the wax seam by pressing the edge into the body of the candle with your warm fingertips or by using a hair dryer, which is easier if the room or your hands are cold. Don't go overboard and melt the wax—only soften it gently and press it together.

Molding in Cans or Molds

Candles can also be made by melting wax in the top of a double boiler and pouring it into a special mold. This means you'll be handling molten wax, and the chances of a mishap rise exponentially. Don't try it with fidgety children until you have some experience with the process via a class or video tutorial.

Dipping

Dipped beeswax candles will burn longer, but the process is trickier. It requires more beeswax, for one thing. You'll need to fill a long container with melted wax—melted again in a double boiler—and then dip a weighted wick into the wax until the desired thickness is reached. The candle is then hung up to dry and cure. Many of us are familiar with this process from living history museums and re-enactor gatherings. It makes very nice candles, once you have mastered the technique, but it can get tedious and is not something you want to try with even the best-behaved children.

Icons: The Broom

Imbolc is a traditional time to replace the household broom. There is much to say about brooms and their uses in cultures all over the world. The modern word comes from one of the dried plants that can be used for the head of the broom coming from the *Genista* genus of shrubs.

Broom replaced the older word *besom*, and some ceremonial brooms are still referred to by that older word.

A broom is a simple, easily constructed, and important part of a homestead, no matter whether that is a large manor house or a tiny apartment in an urban center. There are different brooms for different chores, from short whisk brooms to long-handled warehouse brooms with their wide and sturdy brush-heads.

Legend tells us that the stick or handle of the broom was carefully chosen to fit the hand and the height of the user. If you have ever used a tool day in and day out, you know how important the feel of that handle is—so that when the brush of a besom was worn down to the nubbins, the head was replaced on the comfortable handle.

Witches notoriously travel by broom, and there is sometimes discussion about which end of the broom goes in the front when it is used as a mode of transport. And there's no reason to debate when the broom is used in a bonding ceremony for it lies flat on the ground and the hitched-up couple leaps over it, running into the reception hall ahead of the guests, to share a hug, a kiss, and a quick cold glass of champagne.

When the house receives its new broom, the old one will begin service as the garage broom or the porch broom and continue on a while longer as a vital part of the family. But all good things must fade at last, and brooms, like flags, must be treated with respect upon their final retirement. If made of wood and straw, they should be burned. And you really don't want a broom made of plastic. It won't do a good job when new, and it will age badly. Best to trust the old ways in this case and get a sturdy, reliable, and natural broom.

Season's End

This is the precursor to the great season of renewal that comes in full force with the next Quarter Day and its nesting of Ember Days. This is a quiet season, a gentle unfolding of the possibilities to come. Its Pagan name, Imbolc, comes from a Gaeilge phrase that means "in the belly" and is thought to be called that because it is the time when lambs are born, when there was a collective sigh of relief that there would be ewe's milk for the frail elders of the family, as well as the lambs.

Take some time as you leave Imbolc and venture forward to consider your own frailties, physical, emotional, and spiritual. Ponder the effect of the Winter season on yourself, your kith and kindred, and the land with which you dwell.

Make a list. Make a plan. The time of sharpest rest has reached its natural conclusion, and we venture into the full and verdant spirit of the land itself. Take good care to be as ready as you can reasonably be.

4

The Vernal Equinox:
A Blooming Quarter Day

Chicks and ducklings watch with care,
Check the fencing round their lair!
Plant potatoes, beans, and roses:
Take good tincture for stuffy noses.
Spring is surely here at last.
The weeds are coming on too fast!

Letter from the Forest-Farm: Seated in the Season of Birthing

TODAY, HERE IN THE SOUTHERN APPALACHIANS, the soil is warm enough to do some planting, so I did—onions, radishes, sugar snaps, and artichokes. The potatoes are up and so is the asparagus. Today, here in the Northern Hemisphere, it is the Vernal Equinox, a time of balance—dark and light, fear and courage, work and rest.

I am curiously bright when I sit in my garden, seeds in my pockets, soil under my nails. When my attention shifts back to the media, I feel that frisson of fear and the tightening in my gut. Then I dig my toes into the soil, bring candy to the land spirits, wink at my Ancestors, and thank the Divines.

The Wheel turns. The Great Cycle of Creation and Destruction continues its inevitable rotation.

May the tilt move us closer to light and to re-genesis, to the harvest and to long and lovely days of the waking Earth.

The farm has come roaring back to life! This includes inside visits from outside denizens—mice and ants. The mice are captured in clever little humane traps and removed to other places. I like to think of them as being "rehomed" in a field or copse of trees on the other side of the river. This is a periodic problem in our farm kitchen and best dealt with quickly. My grandmother referred to the tiny mouse-scat as "mice spice." It is unpleasant as well as unwholesome and better off in the woods at the heart of the farm. The ants are dealt with in a far less merciful manner— they are mashed and washed down the drain. This season always sees the migration of all sorts of creatures as they scope out the best places to thrive as the year gears up.

We are behind, of course. Every year sneaks up on us a bit, and we arrive at garden time with still more inside chores to do, the new garden beds not quite ready, and our Winter-achy bodies not stretched out enough for a serious day's work. But we soon adjust—especially to that last bit—and will complain to friends how we hurt in places we didn't know we had!

The strawberry bed seems to have completely disappeared and must be reconstructed this year with more care towards the quality of the soil and more intentional weeding post-fruiting. No sign either of the new grape plant, which was drooping in the Autumn. It is a fact that sometimes plants die and must be replaced and also that attention must be paid long past the planting and harvesting days. We'll look at putting the garden to bed in the chapter on the Autumn Equinox.

These windy, cold days are deceptive. It isn't hot yet, and we think we can get away with not watering those tender little seedlings because it is so cool—cool enough for a jacket because of the fiercesome wind. But the insistent wind will whip the moisture right out of the topsoil, I promise you. Even though the wind will blow you down, go out with the watering can and drench those babies or you will never get caught up with the watering and they will be permanently disadvantaged.

This Embertide: Green Fire

The Second Ember Day in the agricultural year is redolent of rebirth and newness and extraordinary possibilities. We have named it Green Fire on account of the quickness that flows through the land. The Ember Days are times out of ordinary time in which Nature invites us to use the energy of the changing season to renew our own spirit, and we like to use it to think hard about our spiritual practice and see if we are doing what we think we're doing—because sometimes we think about doing our spiritual practice (or maybe feel guilty about it) without *actually* doing it.

If you have been relatively constant in your practice, use this Green Fire to light up your energy and brighten up your outlook. If you've been cruising and maybe slacking since the Winter Solstice, now is the time to take stock of what you used to do and see if it still works for you. Do you want to take something away that no longer brings you into a clearer connection with the Earth? Or do you like what you're doing but want to add in that interesting thing you tried at Imbolc on a more regular basis? Now is a very good time to think hard about what is green and growing—or has that potential—and what needs a good pruning.

Many Pagans prefer to think of setting intentions instead of old-fashioned praying, but I find the two things are not mutually exclusive. I can sit and settle in at my altar and go inside myself to access needs and desires. Time then to set the intention that some of those needs are ripe for manifestation. This may lead me to touch on the immediate needs and set an intention of meeting those here in these Ember Days. If I work with the Divines or my Ancestors, I might then bring the matter before the ones I honor and ask for their help.

Feel the magic in your fingertips move up through your arms, into your shoulders, throughout your body and enter your heart.

Take a breath. One more. One more.

Now.

Release that magic back into the world. Into your house and your neighborhood. Into your city and your county. Your state. Your nation.

And into the world. Let that be your work as the seasons change—to re-enchant the world.

Re-enchant the world by touching your fingertips to the earth.

And so it is.

The Wheel turns. The Great Cycle of Creation and Destruction continues its inevitable rotation.

Blessed Equinox, my friends. Let the tilt move you closer to light and to regenesis. To the harvest and to life!

Life. Life. Life.

Skills

Working with Bees

Backyard honeybees are far more complicated than they used to be—and also far more important. These dynamic pollinators, who came to North America with European migrants, are plagued with pests and diseases and with colony collapse disorder, which seems to have several different causes, none of which are simple to rectify.

Keeping bees is a joy, however, and many beekeepers find themselves mesmerized by the comings-and-goings at the hives. There are many good books on modern beekeeping for you to pore over, but the best thing will be to join a local bee club and see if you can apprentice yourself to an experienced hand. It can be an expensive proposition and a sad one if you lose colonies, as you inevitably will.

I learned beekeeping from someone who approached it in a very relaxed manner. We didn't wear protective gear, but we did tuck our pant legs into our socks and put rubber bands around the wrists of our long-sleeved t-shirts, to keep curious foragers from getting stuck in a sting-able place. The amount of smoke from the smoker was liberal, and the dry material in the smoker always included dried herbs like catnip and thyme. The hive is approached slowly and methodically, as the smart beekeeper has thought about the goal of the visit ahead of time. Part of the goal is always to find the queen and ascertain her health and activity. We want to be alert for signs of varoa mites, foulbrood, small hive beetle, and the like—which you will learn all about in your bee club or bee school.

Whatever we are doing in an active colony should be done with care and confidence, and as quickly as possible. Do not dawdle. Go in, achieve your objective, bless them, and close it up.

We are trying something new with bees at the farm. We haven't set them up yet because we have semi-regular bear visits and a bear will tear through a hive in seconds. We are going to try electrifying a ten foot by ten foot dog kennel and putting a couple of hives inside. This should keep the bears out and allow the bees to forage as they will. We have acquired thyme plants and seeds for more thyme to plant all around the hives. Thyme and its natural thymol are believed by some to repel varoa and small hive beetles. It certainly smells good when we step on it or brush against it as we work in our little bee yard.

Bees are important pollinators—that much is certain. But there are many more sorts of pollinators to support as well. Check them out in your region and see what techniques are best to encourage their presences in your field.

Telling the Bees

I learned about this old tradition through my voracious reading habit as a child. It might have been from one of Andrew Lang's fairy tale books or some other source, for we kept no bees in the cove where I grew up. But I understood it to be an important thing for the garden and for keeping peace with the land around you. For those of you unfamiliar, telling the bees is the act of imparting news of the family to the hives of bees that reside in the family gardens and farmyards. We mostly hear about it when it comes to a death in the family: one must let the bees know about it as soon as you can because if they find out in some other nefarious and disrespectful way, they may decide to swarm and decamp altogether. But I also understand it to be speedy announcement of any news pertaining to the family and its well-being.

Always circling back to our kinship with the land we work and on which we dwell, it seems only right that the swift and golden honeymakers should be privy to all the goings-on since they are part of the community of beings that make up a homestead. It also strikes me that this ties in nicely with the way I was taught to approach the hives in the back garden— with respect, calm, and intention. In some cultures, the bees were presented with honeyed water on the birth of a child or shrouded in black at a death.

I tell our bees everything at the little forest-farm, though we are not keeping domestic bees just now. I chatter to the bumblebees, tell dirty jokes to the wasps, ask the news bees (*Milesia virginiensis*) if they have anything entertaining to tell me.

Chores

Tidying Up—Altars and Work-Spaces

Some people have altars everywhere and tend them with great regularity. I am not one of those people. I can sit happily at my cluttered and dusty altar for a good long time before I am inspired to attend to it. I have found that using the Ember energy inspires me to look hard at this meditation space—really a spiritual workbench—that I use and see what's on it. A dried-out rosebud from a blessing a few months back: is that a meaningful reminder of that time that can stay a while longer or did it simply get left there and was not cleaned away? I err on the side of tidy now, so if that works for you, you can find the bits and pieces that have lingered far too long and make space physically and energetically for newness and renewal.

Burden Cloths

We came late to the game with the concept of a burden cloth. It is such a simple idea and a versatile ancient tool. A burden cloth is just that: a big piece of heavy cloth (canvas is ideal), a tarpaulin, on which you can throw a heap of prunings, raked-up leaves, and other garden debris. The corners are gathered up and the whole thing is easily and tidily dragged to the compost pile. And in purely esoteric terms, all of us as we walk through the world, tending to our work and our lives, amass emotional and psychological burdens that slow us down, make us insecure, and keep us from doing what we know we are called to. Every time you prune the old apple tree and drag the dead limbs to the burn pile, take a moment before you gather the corners of the cloth and consider what worrisome thing you can lay down on that sacrificial heap. Wiggle your fingers over it, gather up the corners, and let one thing go.

Darning Eggs and Clothing Repair

We discussed sewing in an earlier chapter, and we'll revisit it here, with some slightly different techniques. As cold weather retreats and we look forward to warmer days, this is a good time to sort through your Winter clothes and take a good hard look at them. Did you wear that sweater? Do you even like it? If you don't like it, donate it. If you didn't wear it because of that worn-out place under the left arm, then it's time to repair it, wash it, and pack it away until next year.

Our grandmothers would have wagged a finger at a body who threw clothes away because they needed repairs, and because most of us have grown up without learning these odd old skills and philosophies, we may be shy about even attempting something we might get terribly wrong.

You can't do this wrong. Acquire a spool of cotton thread and a packet of needles. If you're feeling bold, get a couple of spools, one light and one dark. A decent pair of scissors is also a good addition. In an earlier book, I used the idea of an old-fashioned sewing basket as a metaphor for personal skillsets. You can also use a sewing basket as a receptacle for sewing notions. You can even use a tin of the sort that holds cookies at Yuletide. You want to keep both thread and needles dry—the needles will rust and the thread can rot.

We have hand-turned wooden darning eggs at the farm that came from a junk store on the other side of town. The clerk at the store didn't know what they were, and once we told her, she didn't know how they worked. You may choose to scour your thrifting sites for these sweet old artifacts but darning socks without them is easy as pie.

Remember, you can't do this wrong—well, not terribly wrong. Let's imagine that there's a hole in the toe of one of your favorite socks. Thread your needle. Turn the sock inside out. Hold the two sides of the hole together and sew them to each other with stitches as small as you can make them. Tie the thread off in a sturdy knot and trim the thread. Admire your handiwork. Once you get the hang of repairs, you'll keep a basket of repairable items in the laundry room, if you have one. When the basket is full, sit down with a cup of tea and some music playing and make those old favorite things wearable again.

Traditions and Celebrations

All the trappings of the Spring Equinox are available at your local drugstore and art supply shop. We tend to collect baskets at every thrifting opportunity so making a basket of Spring delights is easy and fun. Eggs and candies are standard for Easter, and those traditions are easily transferred to celebrations of the Spring Equinox. Share garden perennials cuttings and baby plants with friends. So many perennial herbs send out lots of new plantlets in the Spring, and it is always nicer to share them—and save friends and neighbors the expense of buying them—than turf them out and onto the compost pile because your garden is overrun with them.

Parades are a popular tradition in many parts of the world at this time. You might organize a parade to show off your Spring finery—including a fancy bonnet—because it is also traditional to wear an outfit of new clothes now.

And don't forget to share a rabbit-shaped chocolate. These are easily purchased, but a simple mold and some melted chocolate squares will make you an instant chocolatier.

Wild Foods: Foraging Opportunities in This Season

So much is available for your wild foods foraging now. Morels are out! Dandelion greens are rich. Violets and chickweed make a good, tangy salad. Wander in the woods and along the hedges with a knowledgeable friend or a good guidebook and see what you can find.

Activities to Do with Children and Other Friends

Natural Dyes

There are plenty of egg coloring options that arrive on your kitchen table as little tablets in a cardboard box—the sort of thing many of us know from childhood. But we love to play with natural dyes in the farm kitchen, and what better thing to play with than boiled eggs to celebrate Spring?

You may have some of these things in your pantry right now, but they are easily acquired in your backyard garden, at the local tailgate market, or within the grocery store. It's fun to remember basic color theory, too. Yellow and blue make green. Blue and red make lavender. You can practice these combinations after you've mastered the dyeing technique.

> Yellow (4–5 tablespoons ground turmeric)
>
> Orange (4 cups yellow onion skins)
>
> Pink/red (3–4 cups chopped beet root)
>
> Green (turmeric dye then cabbage dye)

Blue (3 cups chopped red cabbage, soaked overnight in the refrigerator, or 3 cups blueberries for a different shade of blue)

Lavender (cabbage dye then beet root dye)

Brown (strong black tea or coffee)

How to Boil an Egg

Don't feel silly if you don't know how to do this. Lots of people are unsure of how long the egg should cook, and they end up with rubbery or runny eggs. But it is easy. Put the eggs in a medium-sized saucepan and cover them with cold water, enough water so that the eggs are about an inch below the surface. Put the lid on the pan and bring the water to a dancing, rolling boil on high heat. Keep an eye on it so the pot doesn't boil over. Turn the heat down a bit and let the water bubble gently for seven minutes.

You'll need five or six wide-mouthed canning jars, some tongs, and a cooling rack with a bed of rags underneath to catch the drips. We make each color separately, so expect to spend several enjoyable hours playing with colors.

In a medium-sized pot—preferably an enamel one—combine one quart of water and three tablespoons of plain white vinegar. Bring this to a boil and add in the ingredients required for each color. Lower the heat to low-medium, and let it all simmer for about half an hour. Given the ingredients, your kitchen will smell like soup.

Strain the dye water and add to one of the canning jars. You may choose to wear plastic gloves for the next part—especially with bright and staining turmeric. Add your pre-boiled eggs and let them languish in the bath for at least thirty minutes, longer for deeper color. Rinse out the pot and start the process again for the next color. You will get very good at multitasking the egg dyeing. When the eggs reach the color you want, pull them out with the tongs and set them on the rack to drip dry. For the richest color, leave eggs in the dye water overnight (put them in the fridge).

A word about brown: It seems silly to color a white egg brown when you can simply buy brown eggs. But the look of a tea-dyed egg is different from the lovely brown eggs your Rhode Island Red hen lays so faithfully. And they are perfect for creating the varying skin tones of your diverse friends when you're making portrait eggs, which we'll outline now.

These natural dyes can be used to dye things other than eggs, of course. Yarn and paper are especially easy.

Egg Babies

My grandmother kept a small package of colored pencils in the top drawer of the buffet in the dining room. These were used every year at Easter to make what she called "Easter egg babies." These were boiled eggs dyed a pinkish color and then decorated with faces courtesy of the colored pencils. It was always a special time—usually a Saturday afternoon—when she boiled the eggs in her odd electric egg cooker and got the tablet-and-vinegar dyes ready in heavy white stoneware coffee mugs. We wore old t-shirts and dyed every egg that came steaming out of the cooker. The eggs cooled on ragged tea towels, and we got the dining room table ready for drawing the little faces. My grandmother did most of them and the ones she did had wide eyes, long lashes, and little bow mouths. The ones I did looked much the same.

In the farm kitchen, we make little portraits of friends and family to give away. Spirals of curly hair and green eyes for one friend, no lines for hair for our shaven-head friend. You get the idea. Do one for each person in your family, whether your blood or chosen family. Do one for the dog and the cats. Finish the eggs by rubbing them with a tiny bit of butter or oil.

Icons: Eggs and Rabbits

Eggs symbolize life the world over. For Easter, the Greeks do beautiful red ones that are baked into braided breads. As you work with eggs during this season and in the months to come—when our cheerful hens announce the arrival of this perfect food every morning—remind yourself that many beings—ourselves included—begin as eggs. When our creative juices are flowing, ideas begin as their own sort of egg and take on heft and shape as they mature in our brains.

Rabbits have the reputation of excessive breeding, adding to their numbers with frequent birthings of large litters of kits—up to ten. They may be associated with Easter and Spring in the United States because of the Oster Haws traditions that came here with German immigrants in the eighteenth century.

Season's End

We have added richness and color to our lives, just as the Earth has added color throughout the blooming yards and blossoming woodlands. There is much to do and to consider, but it is also an important time to sit and simply *be.* Throughout the turning of this beautiful Wheel, never let a season pass you by without taking time to connect with the meaning of the time, for both the human cultures that form us and the spiraling energy of the world moving towards the magic and vitality that are so beautifully encompassed in the next season—lusty, hungry Beltane.

CHAPTER SEVEN

Summer:
The Waning Year

Beltane

Midsummer Solstice

Lammas

Autumnal Equinox

5

The Season of Beltane: Dancing Life

When Beltane strides onto the field—
With basket of seed and promise of yield—
Beware the bite of summer storm.
Give thought to seedling newly formed.
Look forward now to sun-filled days
But plan for shade midst harsher rays.

Letter from the Forest-Farm

IT IS A FINE APRIL DAY, nearing the end of the month and the complex season of Maying. Isn't that a funny old word: *Maying?* This time of year holds so much richness for all kinds of people, but the names we associate with it sometimes put people off, especially those who use a specific word for it. I also like that it is a verb, an action word, because this season is a season of doing, of "going it."

We have swept the front porch and scraped the last of the soil into the yard. The last two days we have been filling up window boxes and hanging baskets. We'll explore this fertile season that we call Beltane, and we will look at the coming of Summer to the forest-farm. For our purposes of looking at the Wheel of the Year, we will adhere to the notion of Beltane as a Cross-Quarter Day that encompasses a period of about six and a half weeks.

In the southern highlands of the Appalachian Mountains, we have several cold spells in the midst of the warm-up of Spring. We call them "Winters," and these swift cold snaps almost always occur in conjunction with natural phenomena. As the dogwood trees begin to bloom—generally around mid-April—we experience Dogwood Winter. The final mini-winter occurs at the first of May, at Beltane, and it is Blackberry Winter since that's when the brambles bloom.

It can be challenging to convince cloaked and shivering participants that Beltane begins Summer when the temperatures are anything but warm. Sometimes kicking in the doorway of Summer involves a light frost, freezing or near-freezing temperature, and even a light dusting of snow in this part of the country. The same willful weather patterns will make an appearance at the Hinge on the opposite side of the Wheel. The weather's confusion often mirrors our own as we tread the stepping stones between seasons, unsure if we can dance or are safer plodding in our wellies.

We have the expansion of the Beltane holy day through the "Strange and Savage Proposal"—in the second essay on Tower Time and the Conceit of the Ever-Turning Wheel—that invites us to stretch out this season by adding in Rogation Day, Arbor Day, and Earth Day. The feast is laid before us—what shall we do with it?

In many Pagan traditions, Beltane is focused on flower crowns and lust. But there is so much more to this robust and extravagant liveliness. Think about your life and observe the world around you. Walk on the land, whether it is your own woods or an urban park. Breathe in the air. The pollen may still be yellowing all surfaces in its desire to make new plants, or your pollen season may have eased off. Plants are fierce lovers and effective breeders when left to their own devices, even when they seem to be looking for love in your sinuses. When we marvel at all that plant lust, we can consider how we express our own love in the world, for the world, and for the land with which we dwell. Maybe you are holding back because you have been hurt too much. You may be socially sensitive to looking silly, if you show how crazy in love you are with the trees and the exquisite radishes in your garden. All of that—and however you feel—is alright.

When you are able to fall in love with the azaleas and give your heart over to the colors and the millions of blossoms, you can set aside worry and fear for a moment as you live in and breathe in the beauty and the life of your azalea kindred. There can be peace there, if only for a moment. And your understanding of the function of those flowers and the pollinators moving through them—things that have nothing to do with you, that go on whether you observe them or not—imparts a sense of wonder that our daily lives can often overlook, thinking we don't need it. Wonder, like enchantment, is an animist's way of embracing our true role in the webs of life. Sometimes we are active participants, sometimes we are observers—all times have value and are sacred. Each of those holy moments brings us one stitch closer to repairing our ragged souls.

Those plants that are too-often labeled weeds are stubborn in their growth and willful in their habits. These hardy perennials, like plantain, dandelion, and mugwort, come back year after year, defying all but the strongest pesticides. We can think of that as a lust for life, but it is more rightly the strength and power of the life force itself and the desperate need to reproduce and continue the species at all costs. Those plants show us some things about ourselves. We can consider what we are stubborn about and whether that serves us. How often do I give up when the thing I am doing feels too difficult? There are things in my life I will go to the proverbial wall for—my family, my work, my community. There may also be things I've clung to for years and am realizing only now how unimportant they are in the scheme of my life. Observing the rebounding life of a single dandelion plant can be a springboard to making necessary changes in our habits and to the revelation that we aren't at all who we used to be or who we thought we were. That affords us the chance to create or recreate a life of meaning and authenticity.

Our lusty Maying encompasses planting, eating perfect radishes, and wrapping life around us like a cloak of hawthorn blossom. Here on the little forest-farm, we are giving ourselves a long and almost leisurely celebration of Maying in all its variety and sweetness.

Skills

Brewing

Years ago, I sat on a friend's porch and lamented the fact that I had to go home and make grape jelly. The friend asked if that was a particular favorite, and I told her that we had a bumper crop of grapes and this seemed the logical thing to do with them. She gave me a strange look and asked, "Why don't you make wine?"

Supposing that my household would be more likely to drink five gallons of wine than consume an equal amount of grape jelly, I started researching. There was some equipment to consider—a five-gallon plastic bucket with a lid, a carboy (a heavy bottle with a narrow neck that is used for fermenting), airlocks, yeast, sugar, and all those grapes. That first batch of wine was tasty, and I now make wine anytime I have a surplus of grapes. (I have also made red currant wine, and it was finally drinkable after five years of lying about in the cool basement.) That early success emboldened me, and I went on to do hard apple cider and, lastly, beer, including some light herbal ales. All of them have been drinkable, some more than others. I borrowed the equipment the first time out because it can be a bit expensive to start. But I soon found that brewing goes through fads and finding lightly used equipment isn't difficult at all. Our town has an excellent brewing supply store. The owners and staff are a wealth of information and helpful when you are starting off. Look for a class in your area to get you started or borrow all the gear and go with the old trial-and-error method. Either way, it is well worth the effort. Homemade alcohol also makes unique gifts for your friends who imbibe.

Soap-Making

Soap is so ubiquitous we hardly give it a second thought. It comes in solid and liquid form and is inexpensive and available in all kinds of shops. Soap and water are transformational tools, making the unclean clean again, salvation in a bar of foaming, bubbling oils.

Soap-making is a craft worthy of study and perfecting, but you may be best to start with blocks of soap base from the craft store. It is melted in a microwave or the top of a double boiler and then poured into silicone molds. There is no mixing required unless you are adding color or fragrance. Using soap base means you don't have to work with lye, which is an essential part of soap-making and also caustic and tricky to use. Start out the easy way and work yourself up to more authentic processes. Or find a soap maker in your area whose product appeals to you and support their work.

Chores

Flea Beetles and Number Ten Cans

One destructive garden pest easily foiled is flea beetles. They eat holes in the tender leaves of new plants and compromise the ongoing health of your garden. You can surround each of those tender youngsters with a metal can. The large size that works very well for this is a Number Ten can. You can find them at restaurants—they hold food as diverse as tomato sauce and pineapple chunks. A Number Ten can carries about a gallon of liquid product. Wash the cans and let them dry, then remove the bottoms with a can opener. Peel off any paper labels and put those in the recycling bin. Place the cans around your plants to be removed once the plant's stem is a little tougher or leave them on throughout the season.

Vermiculture

The beauty of rich and fertile soil is the partial responsibility of the mighty and humble earthworm. Your compost as well as your planting beds should be a home for them, but you can never have too many of them in the garden. They are part of the phylum Annelida and easy to raise—which is called vermiculture—to add to your garden. You can get kits at any good garden center to get you started. A small earthworm farm can live happily under your kitchen, feeding off your kitchen scraps—though the thought of that might not thrill you.

Walking the Bounds

As daytime lengthens, there are a number of chores that require our attention. Before the growth gets ahead of us, it is wise to walk the fence line and make necessary repairs. If we wait until warmer and drier weather, the wildlings like honeysuckle, Chinese wisteria, and Japanese knotweed will be ahead of us, discouraging us in our determination to keep the animals on the appropriate side of the property line.

It also reminds us of the delightful and sometimes difficult tradition of "beating the bounds." This activity predates the Norman Conquest of Britain and consists of a number of village folk—often led by the mayor or the parish priest—who stroll around the boundaries of the village to ask for good luck and prosperity for the village—and to show the next generation where the boundaries are set. In my beloved Scottish Borders, the same ends are achieved with a celebration called a "common riding," where the boundaries are followed on horseback. My next research excursion to the area will be set to coincide with the Langholm Common Riding. Beating the bounds is also practiced in several areas of the United States, notably parts of New Hampshire and Massachusetts.

My old friend Robbie Sweetser gets his sturdy bike out every May Day and rides the city limits of our town to beat the bounds and mark his presence in the history of the place. This is an act of reclamation as well as attachment, and he delights us with stories of whom and what he sees as he goes about this sacred and magical act.

When you are determining to repair your fences and walk the property line, I recommend you do this activity with friends. Pick a day with decent weather, promise good food and your high-gravity hard cider, and provide the necessary tools for repairing the type of fencing you've installed. Many hands really do make light work when it comes to chores like this. And just like those elders in English villages who are imparting important information to the next generation, you will be showing your less experienced helpers an important skill.

As you beat the bounds of your property, the canny Pagan farmer will also renew the wards that energetically ring her piece of heaven in a stout line of protective magic. I usually leave a physical talisman as I walk the land's edges. You should use something that will not be affected by inclement weather. Stones are good—I would paint them with eye images to double up protection. I also like those flat-bottomed glass beads that florists use in cut arrangements. Drop them at intervals as you check the fence line and tie the grid in place energetically when you've finished the mending chore—and before you down that first cold cider!

Bees

You installed your new bees last month and fed them well to get them established in their new home. They have been learning their territory and visiting the Spring flowers that yield such light honey—apple and cherry blossom, dandelion, early hellebores. At the forest-farm, we eagerly await the imminent arrival of the poplar flow when those delightful trees produce the orange and yellow tulip-like flowers that give them their name. Your bees will redouble their efforts, and the queen will be well-fed as she pops eggs into those perfect larval cells to replace the workers that are soaring away from the treetops, their saddlebags filled with gold.

As you check your hive bodies, keep a good eye out for the position and health of the queen, as well as scouring the place for those dangerous invaders varoa and small hive beetle. If you are in an area with pesky black bears, test the strength of your bee yard fencing, too, making sure the electrical components—whether solar or provided by the power company—are what they should be to deter this Vogon Constructor Fleet from your bees. An average-sized bear can wreak havoc in a few hours while you are at the tailgate market, destroying your investment in both stock and equipment.

Mowing

Mowing begins in earnest now, which is as good a reason as any to get rid of whatever lawn you may have left. There is a hand-operated push mower at the farm that takes care of the paths between raised beds and the area under the clothes line. It uses no fossil fuels, is moderately efficient, and also makes for good exercise. They are generally available at hardware stores and building supplies centers, but be sure to check your local thrift stores and ads for the ambitious person who bought one only to discover it was too much work. Those mowers go fairly cheaply because your bargain purchase alleviates the original owner's guilt.

Livestock: Chickens

With growing hours of sunlight, your flock has begun to produce eggs after the Winter rest. As with most things this time of year, take the time to make sure their houses, runs, and chicken tractors are prepared and clean. You may have had some loss over the Winter, either through illness, depredation, or Sunday supper. There are opportunities now to add to your ladies' numbers by incubating fertilized eggs or buying chicks. Please check the varieties available to get the right chickens for your needs. Do you want friendly hens that get broody and reward you with nutritious brown eggs? How about fancy strutters with wonderful feathered hairdos? Do you want eggs with pastel-colored shells? Consider what is best for your smallholding and your schedule and purchase accordingly.

Avoid at All Costs the Seduction of Easter Chicks

The sign at the feed and seed store announces the arrival of chicks, ducklings, and turkey poults. Unless you are genuinely ready to either begin poultry husbandry or add to your existing flock, you must resist the urge to come home with "pockets full of chicks," as one friend quipped recently. Poultry, like any livestock or animal companion, requires thought as well as preparation. Do you have a henhouse or chicken run or the ability to put one together tout de suite? Because those wee and pooping bundles of fluff cannot live indefinitely in the cardboard carrier from the feed and seed store nor in your bathtub. A half dozen adorable ducklings will soon become a messy and sometimes aggressive mob of animals that may have imprinted on you and follow you about in an increasingly demanding fashion. Ducks are water birds. They need enough water to swim about in—a pond, not a child's wading pool.

If I am making this sound like no fun at all, that is my intention. Poultry is a valuable addition to any smallholding, and I do want you to consider them. Eggs warm from the hen are delicious as well as nutritious, as are large, richly yolked duck eggs. But poultry must be given the same level of consideration as any livestock. Most of us would be unlikely to bring home a calf or piglet without learning all we could about care, feeding, housing, and health care. Poultry requires the same. Give yourself every advantage for being a good poultry herder, and the rewards will be many.

Traditions and Celebrations

Make time and plans to enjoy the movement of change in this time before Midsummer. We dress our modern Beltane in the trappings of folkloric

May Day—paper cones filled with flowers and left on a neighbor's door-knob, washing our faces in the morning dew, drinking crisp May-wine, and dancing the ring.

If you are blessed with children in your life, Beltane is an excellent time to reinforce body positivity, too. Ungainly, shy, or round children almost always benefit from executing simple circle dances with their companions and family. Some of us grew up with the notion that washing our faces in the first dew of May Day guaranteed a lifetime of beauty, giving the canny parent and grandparent a chance to reframe what beauty means in a toxic culture that narrows the definition of that old and sacred concept. Or the dew can bring about strength or good health or foster a connection to the beloved land. Broaden the original concept, Pagan-style, by expanding the idea of beauty in creative ways.

Old-fashioned neighborliness is making a comeback in this too-fast and too-busy culture. Let your Pagan sensibilities guide you as you add these fripperies to your Beltane celebrations. Sneaking over to your elder neighbor's house and hanging a basket of flowers on the door is a delight for children and, frankly, for us oldsters, too. Leaving a potful of pansies on the porch of a new mother will lift everyone's spirits.

Wild Foods: Foraging Opportunities in This Season

This is the time to gather in medicinal and edible herbs. Plantains, broad-leaf and narrow-leaf, are making a very good show now. Consult with your local herbalist for lessons in which plants do what and book a plant walk to learn more.

Activities with Children and Other Friends

Flower and Ivy Crowns

Some of the sweetest images of this season involve children with cir-clets of flowers in their hair, but we know that a circlet of greenery is a compliment to any head, in any season. Fresh greenery and flowers are the best, but a durable circlet of silk leaves and flowers is another consideration. Soft pipe cleaners make a good base, if braided together, and are comfortable to wear for all the activities the Beltane season offers. Fat necklaces and bracelets of flowers are also a fine addition to your Beltane wardrobe. There cannot be too many flowers in this fecund and seductive season.

Posies on Doorknobs

So much of what I have written about in these pages and that I teach when I travel is about building and strengthening communities and our interpersonal relationships with the people that live in our neighborhoods. We tend to have social groups that require going to different parts of town for visits—and even to different parts of the country.

Most of us live in some sort of place where there are neighbors: people whose houses or apartments are near the place where we bide. As the culture around us changes and as we change, it will become more and more important to know the people who dwell in those places. This can be challenging because our societies no longer credit the importance of this sort of interdependence and we can find it difficult to establish relationships with strangers, even if they live on the other side of our fence.

An old tradition of neighborliness that has been part of the Maying season is the creation of posies, nosegays made of little flowers and Spring herbs bound together with narrow ribbon. The nosegay is set into a paper cone with an affixed handle that can hang on a doorknob. They are supposed to be given early on a May morning before anyone else is awake, but it is perfectly fine to warn the recipient that the gift is on its way so it doesn't wilt on the front door of people who always go in and out of the house another way.

If you don't know your neighbors and are squeamish about hooking a posy onto someone's door that you're not sure will be receptive, start with people you know who live nearby or with family members, whether birth or intentional. You may discover the courage to give one to your distant-seeming old neighbor who doesn't seem particularly friendly. You may be pleasantly surprised by their reaction.

Icon: The Maypole

Iconic, terribly traditional, and exuberantly phallic, the maypole is often danced ineptly but always enthusiastically. The tradition is not as old as we've all been led to believe, but that doesn't make it any less dear or important.

Let's look for a moment at a little-known chapter of American history and a flawed but fascinating American figure, Thomas Morton. He and his merry band of miscreants erected the maypole at Merry Mount, a place and event that was not included in your seventh-grade history textbook.

We know his story from Nathaniel Hawthorne's short story "The May-Pole of Merry Mount," published in 1832, though we glimpse it in the work of other writers, notably Washington Irving and Henry Wadsworth Longfellow. The history of the place and events was penned by Morton himself, years later. "New English Canaan" paints an idyllic picture that we suspect now was largely propaganda.

Ma-re Mount was a trading station near modern-day Quincy, Massachusetts. It was remarkable for the time that Morton and his men were respectful of, co-habitated with, and learned from the original inhabitants of the area, and Morton himself wrote of the flora and fauna of the land with real enthusiasm and reverence. In 1627, the colonists at Merry Mount "did devise amongst themselves" a spectacular May Day event that included food, drink, and the erection of a proper maypole, a "pine tree of eighty foote long," decorated with a wreath of flowers and ribbons. (Quotes from Morton's pamphlet "New English Canaan.")

The revels went on for several days but ended abruptly when the Puritans next door—who had had a bellyful of these "pagan" shenanigans—snuck through the woods, arrested Morton, and cut down the pole. The experiment in tolerance was over, and Morton was jailed. He died a few years later, alone, impoverished, and far from Massachusetts. Imagine an American experiment that began not with the restrictions of Puritan-dominated New England, but with the freedom and joy of Merry Mount and wonder where we as a nation might be now, centuries later.

Living the fullness of a nature-centered existence includes honoring the movement of life as it cycles across and through the land, whatever land you are calling home. In this time of sprouting seeds, of not enough rain or drenching floods, our deepest lust can find expression through ceremony and relationship. Embracing the totality of this extraordinary life force that permeates and animates us may be the only thing that stands between our continuation as a species in this unique biosphere—and the abyss. Cultures of despair and death surround us, draining our courage, stifling possibility. In this season of hatching and blooming and planting, we can draw solace from the rolling cycles of time and our intimate connection to it.

Season's End

At this point, we have six more weeks of increasing light. It is difficult to believe as we flow into the heights of Summer that our fate is to witness the start of the waning of the solar year. We are in the time of tending now—of crops and the land that sustains them, on community and on self. Think well on what is needed for this tending and ponder the concept of being tender as well as being one who tends. What is this care that we can lavish on all those aspects of the Summer season and how can we model the acts of tending for those who do not know it?

6

The Bright Solstice: Midsummer

Sun so high in sky so blue
Don't let weeds get the best of you!
Mulch and wat'ring now prevail,
Dream the harvest—do not fail!
Dance now, too, on longest day
Life is sweet with work and play.

Letter from the Forest-Farm: Seated in the Season of Plenty

I'M WRITING ON THE LONGEST DAY OF THE YEAR, which sounds silly because every "day" is the same length. The Summer Solstice marks the most daylight time we can enjoy over the course of the year. Sunset is hours and hours away from sunrise, which gives gardeners time to do our work and children more time to play "before dark." As celebrations go, Midsummer invites us to revel in plenty—enough light, enough fresh and available food, enough time to enjoy outdoor pursuits. In many countries, the children are off from school for many weeks in the Summer, which we understand was originally necessary because they were needed as unpaid farmworkers at that time—something that is still true for many children. It has become a deeply entrenched part of the American year—a time defined by the light of the Sun.

As we strive to root our spirituality into the cycle of the seasons, Midsummer offers us so many opportunities for gratitude and delight. Even for those of us who seem to always carry the weight of Samhain in the center of our souls, this season invites us to use the light to examine things in detail because the brightness helps us to see, literally and figuratively. It is a time to examine the small things, to practice slow-seeing— something we discussed in the Bedrock section.

When your life's schedule permits, sit in the sunshine and ponder the little things around you. This examination can happen outside or at a bright window for those of us who require care in the glare of the Summer Sun. Start with a little thing near at hand: the wasp pecking at the window, the fur of the cat in your lap, your hands, your child's toes. Let your eyes soften and allow your mind to rest, and then to wander. Let your soul be your microscope as you explore textures, colors, and the play of shadow and light. Breathe all the way to the bottom of your lungs and slowly exhale, watching the way your breath moves the cat's fur. Note the shape of the wasp's body and the colors of the wings. Become an expert in this moment on the small thing in front of your eyes. Let your eyes travel over the curves, the lines, the richness of a pattern you don't often take time to notice.

Small-seeing. Slow-seeing. Allowing your eyes to rest on an object in such a way that you really do see it, perhaps for the first time. Try this with a strawberry in this warm and delicious season. Smell it. Note the color and how the hue changes. The texture of its leafy cap is quite different from the smooth but pocked body of the berry. Hold it close to your face and you can see the seeds stuck in their red caves. Nibble the tip of the berry and hold that piece in your mouth, on your tongue. Feel the moisture of it, taste it. Now bite the berry in half and twist the cap into a handle so you can eat the rest. Savor the texture, the flavor, the wetness.

There will be time to turn this bowl of strawberries into jam and topping for shortcake. For now, this one berry is yours, and you also belong to this berry. For this one perfect moment, in the midst of so much light, you have leave to see the totality of the berry and your relationship to it. You have leave to acknowledge your kinship with the food you eat and to wonder at a kinship that is based on sustaining each other in the web of living. You eat that berry. Your body processes it, and the seed comes out of you, ready to do its work. In modern settings that seed may be from a hybrid and will not reproduce. In addition to that, you are likely to deposit that seed into a chemically enhanced sewage system where it won't get the chance to sprout in soil.

As the long day rolls on, consider that, too. In our industrialized world, we have removed ourselves from so many biological processes. In the case of communicable diseases, this is a very good thing. But our intentional separation from the patterns of nature has also left us bereft of the kinship we, as mammals, yearn for.

The salad tomatoes are starting to come in and we must pick the green beans every day to encourage continued growth. We observe the biological processes inherent in this beautiful and vital season by walking barefoot in the yard, picking cucumber beetles off the twisting vines, and eating fresh and raw foods that seem to bring our souls into perfect alignment with the height of this bright season.

With the Quarter Day comes another Embertide, a time to intentionally recharge our energies as well as our spiritual practice. This is the hottest Ember Day, energetically and temperature-wise. We are calling it the Embertide of Tall Corn, which may remind you of one of the songs from the musical *Oklahoma!*, which glories in corn as high as an "elephant's eye."

In my personal practice, I use the Full Moon to recharge my energetic and spiritual batteries, and I approach this long Sun-filled time in the same way. The planting season is finished for the most part—oh, there are always a few things to tuck into the ground throughout the growing season—and we have fretted over weather, seed germination, pest control, and the thousand other details that will ensure a successful crop. We have also put in many days' work digging new garden plots, erecting or repairing fences, and hoisting forksful of manure in the compost. This Embertide of Tall Corn can be used in much the same way—three days of recharging, of respite and relaxation.

This beautiful long day—like its counterpart on the other side of the agricultural wheel—also marks a pivotal change from the waxing of the year into this lightness to the waning of the year into the season of shadows and mist.

Skills

Dancing

We are fans of dancing here on the farm, and we keep a watchful eye on the ever-growing raised beds in the farmyard. There must be room for the firepit and enough room to dance around it. We have been known to circle the raised bed that holds the exuberant haricot beans, urging them on in their splendid growth.

I suspect humans are born to dance, and there are so many ways to do it that almost anyone can. Those who travel by wheelchair can often dance with their arms and keep time with tapping feet. Those who have often been told they are awkward or clumsy are invited to move slowly and steadily, doing simple steps to catchy tunes. Many of us are shy about moving our bodies about in public and can achieve some confidence by dancing alone at home or in our back garden.

The key to confident dancing—once you've gotten your courage strong and your sense of fun polished a bit—is to take it slowly and do something simple with people you like. Circle dances are enjoyable and easy, and you can do them with as few as three people. Start with moving together in the same direction. When I visited my daughter's school at Beltane, I'd teach the class a simple circle dance. We would start by having everyone put their left foot into the circle. There would always be a few who did the wrong foot, and I'd say, "other left foot, please," and they'd change. This also works with adults, by the way, who get flustered and should never be shamed about it.

If you have someone to drum or even clap a rhythm, that is very nice. But the group can do that as they dance, which is only a little confusing and only for a moment. Starting on your left foot, you simply step sideways in that direction, and keep stepping. Clapping or drumming slowly, the group continues moving together until they catch the rhythm and relax into it a bit.

From there, your group may want to take hands, and you may want to vary the steps a bit. As the dancers realize they can move their bodies in space, they will naturally move a little faster and require more complicated steps or rhythms. All in good time—holding hands and circling are such a meditative and community-building act, it is worth it to take a moment and feel confident in the movement. Soon enough you'll master the grapevine step—that you may remember from fourth grade PE class—and be weaving and winking through a spiral dance.

Chores

Weeding

Step one: define a weed. As we become more and more familiar with the native plants that spring up in our yards and gardens, we find that the glorious greenness that you are cheerfully digging out of the path is delicious chickweed and the prolific spearhead leaves over by the driveway are the hallmark of plantain, which is a sovereign medicine for cuts and bites.

A weed is a plant that is growing where the gardener doesn't want it to grow. Anything can be a weed, and so many are edible. The more you garden, the more familiar you will be with all the things that can clutter up your intentional planting bed—and you will know the difference between the sprouts of the seeds you planted and the other baby plants that are taking advantage of your amended soil.

Mulch

Mulch is broken-up or otherwise shredded natural materials that are used to cover bare soil to prevent moisture loss, keep weeds at bay, and give a tidy and uniform look to pathways and growing beds. A thick layer of mulch on your growing beds helps retain the rainwater that your plants need and is advised, regardless of material used. Straw can be obtained at any garden center or feed and seed, but I find it inadequate for my purposes because it too easily sprouts seeds and then I have to weed the walkway. I prefer last year's leaves or shredded newsprint—which isn't very pretty. Many towns have a mulch pile that is the result of citywide leaf pickup in the Fall, and it is available to citizen-gardeners. Your town may also have a grinding service where people clearing land bring stumps to be shredded and the resulting mulch is available for purchase. Mulch is also available bagged up in the local garden center. Small stone can also be used as a kind of mulch but it takes a considerably thick layer to keep weeds down unless you begin by pouring a layer of sand on the paths.

Compost

Compost is the process by which organic material like kitchen scraps and grass clippings becomes soil. It is indeed magic—the magic of microbial activity that is decay and transformation. Banana peels and eggshells break down into soil. Setting up a hot compost pile requires layered materials as well as water and can be seen steaming as the breakdown of material occurs. The heat accelerates the decomposition, getting you that new soil sooner. But even an inefficient pile will yield results—it just takes longer. For urban-dwellers, there are now companies that will pick up your compost bucket of kitchen scraps and return it to you with soil for the garden.

There is a charge, of course, but it is worth it for those apartment-dwellers with green intentions but no land.

Traditions and Celebrations

Thanks to William Shakespeare and older English traditions, most of us can't think of the Summer Solstice without thinking of *A Midsummer Night's Dream* and the faery characters that move throughout that fantastic comedy of errors. Because it is the day with the greatest amount of sunlight, humans throughout the world choose to honor all that light with even more light, with bonfires and fireworks. It is an intense and invigorating celebration of the growing light before we acknowledge that the Wheel has begun to spiral in, tightening its way to Midwinter.

Bonfires

Bonfires mark so many of the special days on the Wheel of the Year, and Midsummer is no exception. Bonfires require a team of sober people who understand the ways of fire. If you go to a Pagan festival, you will encounter fire-tenders with red suspenders who are trained to lay the great fires, to light and feed them, to make sure the bonfire is safe for those dancing around it, and to be very sure the fire is extinguished at the end of its required time. The bonfire at many gatherings holds the very spirit of the event, and there is much anticipation for its lighting, which usually happens on Saturday night as a natural release for the days of excitement and kinship and magic. There are often smaller fires throughout the festival time that culminate in this pièce de résistance.

A bonfire requires a great deal of space. The siting should allow for easy movement around the fire, and this area should have a deep layer of clean sand. A circular seating area can lie beyond the sandy dance area. The persons responsible for the fire should be trained, healthy and sober, and rested enough to stay up until the wee hours, constantly observing the movement of people and of fire. Others may be chosen to keep a close eye on those dancing around the fire lest they get too close and get fire-drunk and erratic.

A covered area for drummers may also be desired and people should be encouraged to bring water bottles or jugs to drink. A terrific bonfire is a deep engagement of the community with all the elements at once, and it is exhilarating.

Fireworks

Such a popular entertainment—the flash, the thunder! Bright and loud and part of commemorative events for centuries, thanks to its creation by the Chinese centuries ago. Most towns of any size put on displays on the civic holidays like the Fourth of July and New Year's Eve. Pop-up fireworks shops appear a few times a year in the parking lots of near-empty malls, and grocery stores have prominent displays.

Most states have very clear laws about the sorts of fireworks that are available to untrained citizen-celebrants. Every year at the Fourth of July, there are reports of children being burned, adolescents losing fingers, teenagers setting fields alight, and drunken people treating the set pieces as though they are not dangerous explosives. If you love to celebrate with fireworks, there are several things to consider: how dry is the landscape, do military veterans live near you, do your neighbors' children or pets freak out at thunderstorms, will the remnants of the set pieces land on people's cars that are parked on the street, are you willing to stay sober and create a protocol for who does what, and, more importantly, who is forbidden to do what?

Parades

Processions and parades are terribly old-fashioned and equally delightful to either participate in or observe. A parade can be a spontaneous affair where you gather up children and dogs in your neighborhood and start at Point A and end at Point B, carrying noisemakers (drums and rattles) and making a merry racket. It can be in celebration of a birthday or other holiday or because the apple trees are blooming or because it is a fine day and everyone could use a distraction.

Processions have a different feel and often are part of a vigil, as we discussed in chapter 2. Processions tend to be more solemn and intentional, but I'd like you to consider a winding, costumed procession through a local park that ends at the picnic pavilion where you share fruit salad in a hollowed-out watermelon.

Sitting a Midsummer Vigil

At the other side of our year's Wheel, we sat vigil on the longest night so that we might sing up the new Sun and welcome the new year. But we stand now at the longest day, and from here forward the Sun wanes to that dark night in December. Can you feel the rightness and the satisfaction of this pattern and how it showcases two bending points in the Wheel, in the same way that Samhain and Beltane balance each other? If you found satisfaction and a spiritual surge when you welcomed the brightening of the year, you may find that welcoming the darkening of the year takes you to an equally significant but different transition. You may choose a night-long vigil as you did before. Or consider going to a quiet wooded place at noon on this longest day and instead of waiting for the dawn, sit in silence, in profound stillness and listening, awaiting the twilight and the arrival of night. If you choose a wood whose paths are not well-marked, don't forget a flashlight to get back through the darkness. But if you sat under your favorite tree in your back garden, try walking back into the house through the well-trod paths without benefit of extra light, embracing the growing darkness as a place of rest, healing, and creative gestation.

Wild Foods: Foraging Opportunities in This Season

The natural world is filled with wild foods and medicines to gather in this bountiful, rich season. Most can be eaten out of hand, following a thorough washing in fresh water. Others will make jams, jellies, and compotes to enhance your breakfast and to share with friends. Here are some of the foods available in my region.

Juneberries

When I was growing up, we called these sweet purple berries "serviceberries." They grow on large bushes, and there is a trend now to see them planted in city parks where they are free for the picking.

Wild Raspberries

Brambles will often make an appearance in the "waste places" in urban areas—the untended hedges and edges of parks, parking lots, and housing developments. Look for them when their small white flowers appear in the Spring and are easy to spot, then check back midsummer to see when they are ripe and ready to pick. North America has wild raspberries, and there is an invasive species called wineberries that are also common.

Elderflowers

Elderberries are blooming now, and their big white flower heads make a healing and delicious cordial. Make sure to leave half of the flowers to form berries in August. The word *cordial* shares its origins with the word for *heart*, and cordials are said to cheer the heart and strengthen it.

Mulberries

It used to be that most neighborhoods boasted an old and spreading mulberry tree whose abundant fruit made thick jams and, after passing through the belly of birds, pink splashes on porches and fence posts. They are untidy trees, and many have been cut down as a nuisance for the homeowner. If you have one near you, check with the homeowner and offer to share your jam in exchange for foraging permission. Most folks will be glad for the bargain.

Lamb's Quarters

This nutritious wild plant is also called pigweed, and it is found in many places. It is good raw in salad and can also be sautéed and tossed in pasta dishes. Don't pull the plant out to harvest it but pick leaves instead. You will be rewarded with cut-and-come-again salad until frost.

Activities with Children and Other Friends

The Sun is decoration enough in these lustrous days, along with the greenness of the natural world. But there is something joyful about honoring the Sun by wearing yellow and golden-hued clothes and buttercup-laden crowns for our heads. We might make a glittery mask with sparkles and sequins, too, to wear for the dancing—because there will be dancing as we turn the Wheel.

Sun Wheels

In this Sun-filled season, you can create pretty window hangings with yellow and white yarn and two crossed sticks. Tie the sticks together where they cross and then use the yarn to wind through the cross, over and under until there's a bright triangle in the center. Hang them on your porch or from tree branches in the garden, and enjoy their spinning brightness as it mirrors the Sun in its fullness.

Sun Masks

Paper plates make masks that are easy to craft and comfortable to wear. You can choose a domino-style mask that covers only the eyes and part of the nose, or you can make a full-face one for smaller faces. The paper is easily painted or colored with crayons or pencils, and sequins and glitter can be glued on to reflect all that sunshine. Use floppy, soft rubber bands at the side to hold the mask onto your ears. Remember though that some people feel claustrophobic in face coverings—especially children—and never force the issue. Face paint may be more fun for some folks and help them bring out the Sun in all of us.

Watermelon Baskets

Put a fresh watermelon on its side and cut it into a basket shape, with a handle on top. Dig out all the flesh with a big spoon and chop it up with other seasonal fruit to make a fruit salad, then dump it all back in.

Icons: The Sun and Fireflies

Somewhere in the mountains near where the little farm lies, there is a once-secret valley, warm and damp. And in that valley during the Summer, there is an occurrence so peculiar that people come for miles and miles to watch it. The fireflies there—insects that we call lightning bugs—blink in unison. It takes them a bit to synchronize and then—blink blink blink.

In Indiana there is a glen with a creek meandering through it. Standing on a wooden bridge late at night, we watch the small movements in the eddies of the water. In our stillness, the lights begin their dance, reflected in the creek. They blink slowly, more slowly than we've ever seen. Calming, mesmerizing—and blue. And green. We stand so long there, lost in this magic, in our wonder.

At the amphitheater where we have come to see another mediocre production of a Shakespeare play, the bug spray is applied as liberally as the wine is poured. Acts One and Two pass as the Sun begins its decline over the western hills. The color is dazzling, and I find it more entertaining than the stage. As the sky darkens, we see them directly upstage of the action—the Sun flying tiny in the trees. The fireflies are manic in their search for love, just as Titania is for her ass-headed lover. It all comes full circle then—the Sun leaving tiny minions in its wake, reminding us that love and light are sometimes as eternal as we wish they were.

Most Summers of my rural childhood, you could find an empty glass jar somewhere in the yard, its lid pierced a dozen times with a sharp nail to create "air holes." This was the bug catching jar, and we were mostly good about our catch-and-release program. I would catch lightning bugs and put them in this peculiar lantern (where usually resided a stick with some drying leaves). When sleep finally overtook me, I brought the jar into the house for the night and set it on the table by my bed. The captives kept signaling for a while, but I was always asleep by the time they stopped for the night. The next morning—after breakfast—they were released into the yard, and the process began again when we remembered it. The revenant Sun in a jar.

Season's End

The giddiness of this glorious season is much enjoyed on the farm where the gardens are planted and mulched and the tailgate markets are loaded with the things we didn't grow. The days are long, and there are music and stories from the porch. Remember. Remember. Now everything has changed, and this carefree joy will soon be transformed to the pleasures of harvesting and the unmistakable feeling that the land is retracting into itself in preparation for the rest it so richly deserves. There will be no rest for us as the harvests come in, but the work is shared as are the prolific zucchini and yellow squash. This champagne-bubble delight—wrap your soul around it while you can.

7

Lammas: The Season of First Harvest

Knead the lump and shape it, dear,
Lammas night is almost here!
Stepping light on holy ground
Dance the circle round and round,
This the harvest, first and fine.
Early wake! It's baking time.

Letter from the Forest-Farm: Standing in the Harvest Season

THIS FIRST IN THE SERIES OF THREE harvest festivals is usually dominated by bread—making it, sharing it, eating it. Some sources attribute the name Lammas to a corruption of "loaf-mass," which makes some sense. The Irish have a festival at the beginning of the month of August that is dedicated to Tailtiu, the god Lugh's foster-mother. It's called Lughnasadh and the month of August in Gaeilge is Mí Lúnasa.

The farm is hot and dry now, and the only place to find any respite is deep in the woods. Even the front porch with its inviting rocking chairs and lush plants is not as pleasant, especially in the late afternoon, as it faces west. We make sun tea on the back porch in the morning and drink it all day long. There are great mounds of lemon balm in the back garden, and its tea is refreshing and oddly relaxing. We are grateful it is so prolific.

There has been food to harvest all season long, of course. Radishes in April, broccoli in May, strawberries in June. But this is the time when harvesting becomes a frenzied activity. There are so many summer squashes, so many tomatoes. I have a confirmed addiction to fresh tomatoes, fresh and warm from the garden. The little salad tomatoes—that here we call "tommy toes"—don't make it into the house. We wipe them on our aprons and pop them into our mouths as we work in the garden or the orchard.

The apple trees are still very young and can hardly be called an orchard yet. We added some bush cherries and a miniature pear tree this year, but they won't bear fruit for several more years. An orchard is a long-term labor of love, and I will probably not live to see it in its full flowering. That doesn't mean I can't see it in my mind's eye in thirty years' time with apples heavy on the branches, soon to be cider and pie and all good apple things.

These are the days of sweat and effort, something many people don't seem to understand or even appreciate. But there is something wholesome about going to sleep with a tired body and a clear mind at the end of a hot workday only to wake after a truly restful sleep and start the whole process again. That sounds dreadful to people who don't work like that, with their hands, with their whole bodies.

Skills

Bread-Making

Yeasted Bread

There was a craze a few years back for bread machines, and everyone seemingly had one for making yeasted breads. I didn't, but towards the end of the craze, someone gave me one. I have never used it: it lives under the buffet in the dining room, still in the original box. I didn't understand the need for a machine, because bread is easy to make and will get easier as you do more of it. I recommend you start with a good flour and fresh yeast, because success early on will embolden you to try all sorts of breads and that is a very good thing. As with most things in life, you should make the sort of bread you like to eat. Some of those will be tricky and will require the bread-making person to be persistent and patient. If you have issues with gluten, there are many good recipes that will yield a satisfying loaf that won't wreck your tummy. There are many types of flour available, and each has its own personality, which will give you the opportunity to have an intentional kinship with that rich-smelling but heavy base ingredient.

Start with a simple white-flour loaf. Find an easy recipe of the sort that invites you to dump five cups of bread flour onto a large cutting board and add some salt, then mound it into a hill. Warm up two cups of water to "bottle temperature." (When women feed babies formula in a bottle and have to warm it up, they test the temperature by squirting a little milk into the inside crook of the elbow. If that feels too hot or too cold, the temperature is adjusted by either putting the bottle back into the warm water it has been heating in or by setting it aside for a few minutes to cool. Hence bottle temperature.) Add half a cup of sugar to the water and stir. Then add a couple of tablespoons of dry yeast. Stir it and leave it alone until the yeast starts to bubble in the warm water. If you have an electric oven, turn it on low for a few minutes. You'll be using it for your proofing chamber. After ten minutes, turn the oven off. It should be cozy and warm but not hot.

With your fingers, create a well in the middle of the flour hill and pour the yeast water into it. Pour in some decent light-flavored olive, maybe a quarter cup. Keep extra flour nearby because you're going to do some of the loveliest work one can do in the kitchen—kneading the loaf. Stir the well with one finger, incorporating more and more of the flour as you stir. Once it has moved past the possibility of run-off stage, use your whole hand to fully incorporate the liquid into the flour. You may need a little extra liquid—that's okay. The loaf should be slightly sticky before you start kneading.

Philosophy of Kneading

Some people swear by doing dough work with only one hand so that you have one "clean" hand to open the oven door or take the teaball out of your teacup. I have tried that and it does keep you from leaving white dribbles in odd places, but my preference is to get into it with both hands, my arms, and my shoulders. It is a marvelous meditative technique as it becomes easy to let your mind wander as you push, roll back, push forward, turn, push forward. Add a sprinkle of flour if it gets too sticky to push. Different flours will require different amounts of kneading. As you practice, you will develop a feel for when the dough is ready to rest. The conventional term is *elastic*, but I prefer to think that you knead the bread until it responds to your touch and feels alive. Then you can step away and put your tools in warm water to soak. When you return to your loaf, poke it with your finger, making a dent about half an inch deep. If it is easy to poke and starts to bounce back and fill in almost immediately, then it is ready to rise.

Add a tiny bit of oil to a deep bowl and rub it all around the inside. With your oily hands, lift the dough, set it into the bowl, and roll it gently so that it has a light covering of the oil all over. Gently rest your hands on it and feel the life contained in it. Bless it and let it bless you. Wrap a kitchen towel over the top and around the bowl and set it in the warm oven. It takes about ninety minutes to rise, and you should leave it alone except for a couple of brief checks to make sure it's doing as intended.

When the dough has more than doubled in size, remove it from the oven and turn it out on a lightly floured board. It will probably have some bubbles and dimples. Smell it. Now punch it down. You aren't kneading in the way you did before. Now you're getting it ready for shaping and baking, so it only needs a quick flattening. If you are using loaf pans, divide the dough into the appropriate pieces—usually two—and place in the lightly oiled loaf pans to proof again. If you are making a rustic and less-structured loaf, shape it on your floured board and slip it into a baking pan. Leave them now for about half an hour. Heat the oven to 450, and place a small pan of water on the lowest oven shelf. This will help your loaves have a firm crust. You may also choose to spray the inside of the hot oven with water to create steam.

When the loaves have almost doubled in size, spritz the oven again. Depending on the sort of bread you are making, you may want to slash the tops of the loaves with a sharp razor blade. Put the loaves in the oven and turn the oven down to 350.

The smell of the bread as it bakes will be seductive and comforting. Most loaves take forty-five minutes to an hour to bake. The loaf is ready when it is a lovely golden-brown color and, if you remove it from the baking sheet with a towel and flip it top-side down, it will sound hollow when you knock on the bottom—like knocking on a door.

Try to be patient and allow the hot loaves to rest on a cooling rack for about ten minutes. This is the hardest part of making your own bread— this waiting business and not simply lobbing it out of the oven and smearing it with butter. Take it out. Put it on the cooling rack. Get out the butter and jam. Make a cup of tea. Find your serrated-blade knife and take out the cutting board.

That should just about do it. Now slice the loaf into fat pieces and smear them with butter or dip them in oil, and have bread and tea—like a civilized barbarian.

A Word about Natural Yeast: Sour Dough

I have always used packaged yeast because it is consistent and readily available, but there are many people who capture "wild" yeast in a variety of ways and have good results. Periodically sourdough starter reappears and is everywhere amongst my foodie friends. One person has a mother (also called a sponge), passes part of it to friends, and everyone starts making sourdough bread. The mother must be fed with flour and water to keep it active. It is delightful to trace the lineage of a sourdough sponge as it moves amongst your friends and neighbors. The proofing time of a loaf will depend on how vigorous the starter's level of bacterial activity is, but it generally takes longer than a loaf risen by commercial yeast. The starter imparts much of the flavor of the bread, too.

Other Leavening: Soda Bread

Soda bread is most often trotted out during the month of March because it is a traditional Irish bread. The recipe I use came from the landlady of the bed-and-breakfast place I stayed in near Kildare. Soda bread can be made with any kind of flour but will be more cake-like if you use a lighter flour. I use half unbleached all-purpose white flour and half whole wheat. It is a fast and easy loaf and can go from taking down the bowl and flour to buttering a slice with your neighbor in a little over an hour. The leavening for soda bread is baking soda, but I use buttermilk for the liquid and that helps the rise as well. It is usually a dense loaf with no layers and a thick, firm crust. If you are doing a gluten-free diet, try other flours until you achieve the texture you prefer. I have tried a low-carb version with almond flour, but it wasn't to my taste.

Chores

Food Preservation

When you grow a garden, there are some vegetables that are ready to eat all at once. It is always the best idea to go to the garden, cut a head of broccoli, clean it, and cook it on the spot. The flavor is best, and the nutritional values are almost as good as raw. Broccoli is one of those crops that tend to all come due at once, so you have a couple of options. You can eat as much as you want and share, sell, or barter the rest. Or you can eat some and preserve the rest.

Canning

It seems such an old-fashioned thing, something we remember grand-mother did in some former and bucolic time. More and more people are discovering the joy of food preservation as more people either grow their own or visit growers at a local tailgate market. It is a skill well worth learning, and the fact is it isn't very difficult. As always, I will suggest that you find a local class to attend to learn the basics. In-person classes will boost your confidence level and introduce you to other people in your community who are also interested in the same things you are, which gives you colleagues as you explore food preservation.

The easiest thing to begin with is jam. It will require jars, fruit, sugar, and pectin. The last item is readily available in most stores, and apple peel will yield the same thing in a pinch. Successful canning begins and ends with clean equipment. Canning jars can be bought cheaply at thrift stores and yard sales. Bring them home and wash them thoroughly in hot, soapy water. If you have a dishwasher, run them through on the hottest cycle. If not, put a big pot of water on the stove, place the clean jars inside, and boil the water.

Canning requires a jar, a lid, and a ring. The jars and rings can be reused, but you should use a new lid for anything that is canned by either water bath or pressure canner. You can invest all the money you saved on jars in buying lids, though they aren't expensive.

Pickling and Fermentation

Many books are available on these two subjects, so I will refer you to other sources for instruction. I do want to share the ease with which kraut can be made in the hopes of encouraging you to jump into the world of fermented and pickled foods. They are delicious as well as nutritious, and the bacteria produced by each have quite a good effect on your gut culture.

Kraut is simple, and I use some of the tools from my wine- and cider-making enterprises when making kraut. Its proper name is *sauerkraut,* which is German for "sour"—and idiomatically "pissed off"—cabbage. It can be made with all kinds of cabbage: The head is chopped up into strips which are placed in a large bowl. Salt is sprinkled on the cabbage, and you knead it until the cabbage begins to release liquid. Everything

is poured into a glass canning jar, and an airlock—from the cider supplies—is screwed into the top. It takes only about a week for the kraut to
be ready to eat. You may can it for eating later or keep it in the refrigerator
to eat within a week or ten days.

Freezing

Freezing is easier than canning, but it depends on having a working
freezer and not having prolonged power cuts. That is a risk many are
willing to take to insure crisper and fresher-textured vegetables. Most vegetables don't require much processing before freezing. They should be
cleaned thoroughly and then chopped into the desired style. Vegetables
freeze most successfully in smaller chunks. Damaged places should be
cut off, and the choice to peel or not to peel is left to the cook. Most
vegetable should be blanched—dipped quickly into boiling water. Then
spread them on cookie sheets and freeze them solid. It is easy then to pop
them off the sheet and into a freezer bag. Label bags with contents and
date. Trust me. You think you'll remember that it's kale and not collards,
but you won't. And you'll be sure you froze those berries last Spring, but
it was the Spring two years back. Label with a black marker and stack in
the freezer until you're ready for them.

Berries are even easier because they don't require blanching. Wash
them, drain them, and pick out the bad ones. Let them drain in a big col-
ander for a few minutes then lay them on a cookie sheet in one layer and
freeze them solid. Into a labeled bag they go; they will make you think of
Summer when you have strawberry shortcake for Imbolc.

Many people are getting away from single-use plastic bags, and that
is a good thing. Sturdy canning jars can also be used for freezing. Choose
the wide-mouthed ones for easy removal. There are excellent recipes for
freezer jams, too.

Traditions and Celebrations

The Blessed Loaf and the Ceremony of Cakes and Ale

There is a lovely ceremony that comes out of the Wiccan traditions. It is called the ceremony of Cakes and Ale and is often a part of handfasting and wedding celebrations. When used as part of a bonding ceremony, Cakes and Ale is a promise between two people to support each other through symbolically offering the other a bite of food and a sip of something to drink. A plate with bits of food is offered, often with the words "May you never hunger." Then the gesture is reversed, and the giver is offered the plate and takes a bite as the new giver repeats the promise, "May you never hunger." The response to that promise is "thank you" or "blessed be," "I love you," or even "yummy!" Then a cup is offered containing wine or water or whatever both enjoy. In the handfasting ceremony, a chalice is used. The promise is "May you never thirst," and the answer is the same as before.

This dear and tender ceremony is more than it seems on the surface. It isn't only about making sure everyone's lunch is packed and the coffee gets made in the morning. It really is a larger commitment about support, encouragement, and assured community. It is a ceremony that could be used more often, in other situations, in my opinion. Again, we see how there can be a literal meaning to all these seasonal observances, as well as a metaphorical one. The Christian Eucharist is a kind of Cakes and Ale ceremony with a promise made through the offering and receiving of a sip of drink and a morsel of food. We might choose to adapt this ceremony anytime we have a gathering with food—Thanksgiving and birthdays come to mind. Anytime you are wrapping ceremony around an event to give it its proper respect and commemoration, consider this powerful set of promises that should be refreshed, whether in a family unit or a larger community.

May you never hunger.

May you never thirst.

May you blessed be.

May we all blessed be.

Wild Foods: Foraging Opportunities in This Season

Depending on the weather patterns where you abide and also on how those are changing as the global climate shrugs under the weight of the human activity it bears, this time of year can be especially dry and hot. Some fruit trees will bear—apples and pears are the most available in my growing zone. Look out in your town and neighborhood for old fruit trees that are left-overs in suburban areas. We are always delighted to see trees that were planted by a previous homeowner and not harvested by the current one. Ask before you take—a good rule in foraging and in life. If the homeowner isn't using the fruit, they may be more than happy for you to take it and to accept the gift of some jars of apple sauce after you've processed them. You are likely to find older varieties of apples and pears this way. Many of the heirlooms have distinctive flavors that we don't encounter in grocery store produce sections.

Activities with Children and Other Friends

Shaping a Loaf-Person

You can make a festive—and delicious—shaped loaf from either a yeasted dough, a shortcrust, or a biscuit dough. The end result will vary, of course, but all will give you a chance to celebrate our human connection to the harvest season by eating something you've made with your own hands. A shortcrust pie crust will give you a relatively flat and crispy fellow. Biscuit dough yields a quick-risen loaf that cooks in no time at all. Yeasted dough gives the best opportunity for ornamentation because it can be braided and easily shaped. Once a yeasted dough has proofed and is ready for the oven, you can continue to add to its beauty. You can roll out a shortcrust pastry and use small cookie cutters to make pretty designs to add to any of these offerings, but roll the crust thinly so that it cooks in the same time as the other dough.

Corn Dollies

There are elaborate braided and twisted wheat decorations that are called corn dollies, and they are an old tradition amongst many cultures. They are often made from the very first stook of wheat and also from the very last one as good luck charms, specifically as protection from fire and lightning strikes. Those thatched roofs we see in some parts of Britain always have a blessing dolly tucked up under the eaves. Dried wheat can be found in most craft shops in the Autumn and must be soaked to soften it enough to braid.

Another choice is to use the shucks that cover sweet corn. They are readily available wherever people love and make tamales. These will also need to be soaked very briefly and then can be braided and folded into many shapes—a drop of glue here and there may also be helpful to hold your creation together.

Picture Frame with Dried Corn

While we're considering the decorative possibilities of this popular grain, I want to harken back to a craft project from decades ago. Girl Scouts did it and vacation Bible school attendees did it too. It requires corn seed—dried corn no longer attached to its cob—and some white glue. A flat picture frame from a thrift shop is a good base, but you can make your own from heavy cardboard. Set your seed out according to color and work out your design if you want something with a pattern. If not, simply put a generous layer of white glue down one section at a time and stick the seeds down into the glue one at a time. You may also add pretty stones, other kinds of seeds, and even sequins to your creation. Allow it to dry flat overnight—or at least for several hours—then put a picture in it. Something you've drawn, a photograph, or a collage or vision board makes it a nice personal statement.

It won't last forever, but it is a charming reminder of a simpler time and maybe a simpler you. This is a good project with children, but I have found that a group of adults, a newsprint-covered table, and some adult beverages can lead to a memorable evening indeed.

Drying Flowers: Flower Press

Children used to press flowers by finding the heaviest book in the house—usually a dictionary—and mashing the specimen right in the middle. That is still a possibility, but creating a press for floral and herbal specimens is usually a better way to go. You will need two squares of quarter-inch plywood eight inches by eight inches, four quarter-inch carriage bolts three inches long with wing nuts, a dozen eight-inch by eight-inch pieces of paper, two pieces of lightweight cardboard of the same size, and a dozen coffee filters. Drill holes big enough to fit the bolts at the corners of both pieces of plywood. Cut the same size holes in the corners of the cardboard pieces. Put the bolts through one piece of plywood with the heads down and the shaft pointed up and lay it flat. Place one of the cardboard pieces through the holes and push it down to cover the plywood. Store all the papers and coffee filters in the press—you can lay them in now. Slide the last cardboard piece over those and put the other plywood square on the very top. Use the wing nuts to tighten everything down. Specimens can be added between a sheet of paper and a coffee filter by removing the top square, adding the specimen, putting the top back on, and tightening it down. The drying time depends on the thickness of the flower, so you can check back every few days to see how it's progressing. When dry, the flattened flower can be removed and used as a decoration on cards and packages or wherever a bit of Summer sweetness is required.

Icon: Wheat

If you read a great deal of English literature when you were young and shirking the chores your parent had set for you—as I did—you may have been confused—as I was—when there was a reference to "corn." They did not mean the sweet corn or maize we Southern children ate with such gusto at this time of year. They were referencing wheat. Hence, a traditional "corn" dolly is made with braided wheat—though I often use sweet corn shucks for the same effect.

Wheat gets such a bum rap these days. So many people cannot ingest it—some can't even be around it—without suffering dire effects in their digestive tracts. We have discovered that excessive carbohydrates have wreaked havoc with the US diet. You may be happier and potentially safer by acknowledging the importance of wheat as a symbol of plenty and as one of the legacies of our human transition from nomads to farmers and pastoralists. One of the symbols of plenty in the Western world is wheat, often placed with vegetables in a cornucopia. We see these in the arms of goddesses that adorn the official seals of many states in the United States.

At the farm, we favor an old grain in the wheat family called Khorasan wheat or Kamut (the product's commercial name). It is big and chewy, a solid grain that we use in tabouli and soup. When I hold a few kernels in my palm, I can sense the history of my species and the plant I'm holding, a saga that begins before the written accounts and is contained in this ancient grain. I imagine a group of women gathering roots and grasses along a creek and finding a stand of this grain's Ancestor—not as fat or abundant but the same basic foodstuff. Did they try it raw first or grind to make a paste? How long did it take them to fiddle with its DNA through hybridization and create the wheat we know today?

Wheat seems to me like a family's homeplace where everyone gathers and remembers the old stories and ways. Holding those kernels feels like an Ancestral homecoming.

Season's End

For anyone who has grown a garden, the idea of the first harvest happening in August seems off because we have been harvesting as the crop in question is ready to be harvested. We have been picking and pulling all season long, from the first French Breakfast radish and wild-gathered chickweed in the very early Spring to today. The *first* of anything gives it significance and an implied history. Instead of laboring under the delusion that nothing has been harvested and enjoyed until now and lamenting that you can't properly celebrate this day because you are sensitive to grains, look to the symbol of harvest and what that means about gratitude in your life—how you express it, how you use it. And it says much about your steadfastness. If you set an intention in the Spring—when we literally and symbolically planted our intentions for the year to come—did you tend it to harvest? Is it ready to feed you now, that thing you imagined planting?

8

The Autumnal Equinox:
A Fruitful Quarter Day

Leaves on trees begin to change,
Fog appears on mountain range.
Time to think of canning food
Or freezing it for winter's good.
Middle harvest, apples bright,
Pressed for cider, sweet delight!

Letter from the Forest-Farm: Grief in a Falling Season

WE ARE ALL WEARY AT THIS POINT in the agricultural year, and there is still so much to do. We have the advantage of so many good things to eat and so many celebrations that buoy up our spirits as we work through this harvest. If we are truly blessed, the weather is cooler, too, which is a glory after the heat of high Summer.

Early apples are coming in, and the gardens are splendid. Several crops must be picked every day to encourage the plants to continue to produce their bounty, and we blanch those quickly and sink them into cold water, bag them up, and into the freezer they go. It is the fate of zucchini, green beans, tomatoes, and the bounty of basil. Basil, to my way of thinking, should be planted along any possible pathway so that it releases its rich scent every time you pass. As a result of this odd obsession, there is always too much basil. It is good to eat fresh with so many things, and it can be whirred in the food processor or blender with oil and salt to become the magical elixir called pesto. This can be spooned into ice trays, released when solid, and stored away still frozen in a resealable bag for the flavor of Summer in the land of Winter.

We seem to spend more and more time on the porch, watching for the changes in the trees, as their green-producing chlorophyll breaks down in the shortening daylight and the cooling temperatures. Birds who have become regular visitors will begin their migrations south, and the ones that stay with us throughout the year are busily fattening up on the seed-heads left for them. Our bear visitor has grown fat all Summer on the land and on the neighbors' trash and will waddle up the mountain for her sleeping-time soon; we wonder if there will be young ones when we see her next.

This Embertide: Wander Days

We have explored Ember Days throughout the seasons. Each of these three-day observations has a different flavor, and the flavor of this one is spiced with wood smoke, bacon, and pumpkin pie. There is a taste of dust in the air as the natural world begins to prepare for its time of rest and renewal. But there is something else riding on the cooling air—an invitation to ramble. I have always longed to travel in the Autumn, and I have found that many people feel the same thing, the same wanderlust.

Travel always gives us an opportunity to be renewed, to see new things with old eyes and then turn around and see all the old things with new eyes. This Embertide is the one in which we gather up all the things we have learned about ourselves, our spirituality, and our acknowledged kinship along the webs of being and incorporate them into the deepest parts of our psyches and souls as we wander the wide world, through time and space, literally and metaphorically. As we walk the road of the year's dying, we are given another opportunity to let go of the things that no longer nurture or nourish us. Leave them like compost along this path so that we face the Great Hinge of the year with expectation and curiosity.

Make Amends from Now until the Samhain Cross-Quarter

The time between the Autumn Equinox and Samhaintide is filled with things to do, with chores as well as celebrations. In many places, the weather has cooled and is very pleasant. It is a time when we can choose to do something difficult emotionally but not physically. I reserve this time in my spiritual practice to take a good hard look at my behavior in the last year. Have I held up my own sense of ethics, followed my own rules of engagement? I consider where and when—and also how and why—I have intentionally inflicted pain on others, when I have been careless and inconsiderate. I consider why I did what I did and whether it was justified.

Then I decide whether or not I can make amends, or at least apologize, and I do that. I also consider whether I feel owed by anyone in my circle, whether money or a phone call or a borrowed book. I take it case by case and let it all go, as best I can. That is the easy part because I don't loan money—if a friend needs money and I have it, I give it. If I have called a friend several times and there's been no response, I make one more call to try to connect and then I let it go and assume it isn't about me or our friendship. When that friend reconnects a month or a year or a decade later, we can still do our catching up with no guilt or shame.

Everyone knows that a book lent is a book given. And that's that.

I highly recommend this as a way to enter our period of rest and reflection without unnecessary baggage. There will be so much to reflect upon between now and the Winter Solstice—release the things that don't require your attention and certainly are not your concern. Now we will be thinking of harvest and the Dead, and that will eat up your attention and your energy.

Skills

Silence and Listening

I pondered where to put this section and settled on it being a skill, one that most of us would be wise to strengthen and that will serve us well if we only practice it enough to become adept at it. Hearing is the act of processing information through listening. Most animals have ears of one sort or another, but some hear through sensing vibrations—snakes and bees do that. Some humans have limited hearing and may choose to correct that with special mechanical aids. Other humans have little or no hearing and are members of a deaf culture that uses a hand and movement-based language system, called sign language, and "hears" by observing the movement of speakers' lips.

Listening is the act of absorbing information through hearing. But it is much more than that. To really listen—to the words of a friend, a musical performance, or the snapping twigs on a woodland path—is to set aside the need to immediately respond and to hold space for understanding to grow.

Silence is relative. If you are standing on the corner of a city street, the absence of car horns blaring or people shouting across the crosswalk may feel like silence. A remote natural area may be very quiet as you enter it, but when the birds and animals get accustomed to your presence, they begin their customary songs and sounds. In nature, silence often means a suspicion of imminent danger.

Silence, listening, and hearing are companion skills that lead us to sources of knowledge we wouldn't otherwise have. Think of that—the kindness of listening to your child or your mate can also bring you wisdom. Everyone benefits.

Chores

Bringing in Houseplants

The houseplants have spent the Summer on the porches, and they are green and healthy. They come inside to the studio room for the Winter, which has a big south-facing window. If your plants are coming in from outside take a few minutes to trim off the dead leaves and other bits. Look on the undersides of the leaves to make sure no outside riders will come along to try to overwinter in the warmth of your house. Aphids, white fly, spider mites—tiny invaders you don't want. Most can be brushed away with a cloth after spraying the leaf with warm water. But for more pernicious pests, you can get a spray at the garden center or make your own with insecticidal soap. Be diligent, but if any hitchhikers manage to get past your guard, take care of them as soon as possible.

As the last of the harvest comes in, the wise thing to do is clear away what can be removed from the planting beds. Okra starts to produce fewer pods, corn is pulled from the stalks and those are removed and stacked together, used for either decoration or animal feed. We like to go ahead and add fertilizer—always manure of some sort—and let it seep into the soil through the rains and snows that will come in the Winter. Your Spring planting and your mood will benefit from doing a little extra work now.

Putting the Garden to Bed

During the section leading up to Midsummer, we considered the notions of tending and of being tender. That is the intention we always set when we are putting the growing sections to bed for the Winter. We trim off all dead and damaged limbs of perennial plants and shrubs. If a plant is bearing seed that is to be collected for next year, those are left to ripen. Likewise, if seeds are a favorite of birds and other animals, we leave those standing for extra calories as they fatten up for the Winter. We like to leave the garden a little ragged until all the plant nutrients have gone into animals or the soil. We won't rake and haul to the burn or compost pile until January, when we prepare the beds for peas and early brassicas. If we are lucky enough to score some animal poop for fertilizer, it gets spread on the growing beds so that rain, sleet, and snow can help it seep into our beloved soil.

Fertilizing and Top Dressing

We discussed mulch and compost in the first chapter, so you know what fine things they are for keeping in moisture and keeping out weeds. As you get ready for the Winter world, you will find it wise to pull back the mulch from many of your perennial plants and put a little composted manure around them, as a top dressing. This will slowly get absorbed as the rains and snows, if you have those, visit the land and give your plants a bite of breakfast when they awaken in the Spring. Don't give them too much, though, or they'll shake themselves awake and sprout when they should be resting.

Wild Foods: Foraging Opportunities in This Season

This is the time of nuts and berries, the delight of bears and wildcrafters. If you have black walnut trees in your region, you know how prolific they can be. Green balls half the size of a tennis ball and heavy as clay will line ditches and create tripping hazards wherever these powerfully magical trees flourish. Black walnuts are a rich and delicious food, and it takes a determined person to break through the green external hull with its slimy black and maggot-ridden interior and then dry the much smaller black nut, which, once dried, is very hard. There are devices to crack these tough shells but most people who love them use a short length of two-by-six board and a heavy hammer. The meat, as with the more refined English walnuts, often comes out in one heart-shaped piece. The meat is oily and strong smelling, reeking of the wild and of poisons and the darkness of the human heart. And it makes a fragrant pound cake and dries easily for use in all sorts of dishes, bringing with it, as it does, the soul of the wild world captured, safe from Winter storms.

At the little farm, we don't pick any berries after the Vernal Equinox but leave those for the four-leggeds, the winged ones, and the land spirits. Depending on the zone, there may still be blackberries, wineberries, kousa dogwoods for fruit and apples, pears, and paw-paws, amongst other foods.

With the usual autumnal coolness—though with climate hijinks, it's hard to guarantee—we often get some needed rainfall, and this inspires the spores in the mycelium world to begin their fruiting. Mushroom hunting is a fine and ancient art, and you would do well to learn it from a seasoned hunter and not wander through the woods with a little book of photos or an app on your phone. There are a few that don't have toxic twins, but it is so easy to make mistakes of the sort you wouldn't wish for either yourself or the people you invite over. Be smart, make friends with a hunter, and spend time in the woods learning the ways of the mushroom people. The rewards are great, but the dangers are very real indeed.

This is also a good time to check your stores of herbal medicines and see what looks sparse in your cabinet. Plantain—the herb, not the banana-like fruit—is still plentiful, and jewelweed is easily emulsified in the blender and put into an ice cube tray to deal with dry skin itches and occasional insect bites.

Traditions and Celebrations

Harvest Home

So much harvesting falls within this season of Autumn Equinox that a celebration of all that richness and goodness seems in order. Americans have an official Thanksgiving celebration that falls in the Samhain season, but those gatherings and feastings have become problematical with their grounding in some of the worst excesses of our nation's history. Many of us will continue those old family traditions, not for their national historical meaning, but because they are a significant piece of our family tapestry. Memories for good or ill are made and relationships woven in these shared experiences in spite of the mythological but historically inaccurate and painful origins. Keep them, if they serve you—roast a turkey, create that weird green bean and canned mushroom soup side dish that was your father's favorite, and sit down for a meal with your awkward and wonderful family. But don't be tied to this if it does not bring you happiness. Instead you may choose to create a special Harvest Home gathering, with either your birth family or your chosen family. Show off your cooking style, order a stack of pizzas, or make it a potluck—the point is to be clear about the earth that has yielded up every possible blessing, to honor with gratitude those who planted, tended, and brought in the harvest—even if that's you. Create a long table from saw horses and hollow-core doors. Throw a clean bed sheet over it or bring out your grandmother's best piece of embroidered linen. Sit with people you love and wipe your happy mouth with a cloth napkin or a paper one or a couple of paper towels. Let the table hold great steaming plates of sweet corn and bowls of roasted Brussels sprouts and pass them from person to person. Show off the callouses on your hands. Drink a toast to absent friends. Eat too much and invite your neighbors to join you.

You planted and ate all the radishes. You ate tomatoes warm from the Sun, wiping your mouth on the tail of your work shirt. You tended what the soil grew for you and you plucked it up. Feel the glory of these simple, wholesome acts. Remind yourself of the power of your extraordinarily ordinary kinship with this biosphere we call home. And ponder what you must owe to this place that holds your past, your future, and your abiding love.

Activities to Do with Children and Other Friends

Tree Cairns

All seasons are tree seasons, but this time when the leaves of deciduous trees color up and fall to the ground is especially good. My daughter and I decided one September that we would give out tree awards. Best color, earliest, biggest—we finally settled on one superlative and picked the one we thought best. The award was a little stone cairn, ideally at the base of the tree. A small pyramid of ten or twelve rocks was stacked into a tidy pile and then we bowed to the tree.

Pressing Pretty Leaves

These Autumn days are often perfect—the temperature is easy, the sky is a soft blue, and any excuse to be outside in it is a blessing. Alone or in company, in a city park or along a dirt road in the county, we step into a world bursting with life, yielding up everything to our mere touch.

Find a basket whose weight is easy on your shoulders and whose handle fits your hand and take it into the Autumn world. Pick the brightest, the largest, the most perfect of the leaves that have given up their hold on the branch that displayed them. Put them in the basket with some usnea and acorns and pignuts. Take them home and press the leaves between two pieces of waxed paper, cover the paper with a pressing cloth or tea towel, and warm the wax until it melts together with the leaf trapped inside.

It isn't permanent. The art you've created as a memory of these perfect days will fade and crumble, no matter how adept you are in the pressing. That is the way of all the world though—to be present in it, hip deep in the wonder of it; that is the soul-memory we can carry, the legend we construct of our place in all these webs of life and of wisdom.

Waxed paper, an iron set on a low temperature, a pressing cloth, and pretty leaves are all you need.

Icons: Labyrinth and Pilgrimage

The wanderlust I and others experience in Autumn can result in actual trips to other lands or other places in your own land. Even if you don't have the resources of time or money to spend three weeks in Tuscany, you can choose a place near your home that you have never visited or one you've spent time in and promised you'd return to. You may choose to keep a journal of the adventure and indulge in that impossibly old-fashioned activity of sending postcards. Most of my fieldwork in Britain begins with a trip to the post office for stamps, the corner store for picture postcards, and then a pint at the nearest pub while I fill them all out. Then I keep a sharp eye out for one of those red pillar boxes and away they go, destined to arrive to the recipient before I get home. I don't have to think of them again and my friends and family know they were on my mind while I was away.

To make a pilgrimage is to travel with an intention other than to be entertained and escape your day-to-day life. A pilgrimage can be to any location that calls to your heart and tickles your curiosity. An old building in your town may be imbued with significance from your childhood or by virtue of its historic significance. Awarding the oldest or largest tree with its own stone cairn is a pilgrimage. The ancient monuments erected by the First Nations people are places of special reverence and power. Approach them with some foreknowledge of their significance to the people who built them, the people who may still tend and venerate them, and how we suppose they were used when first constructed. When we approach places as well as people with respect and affection, there is much that we bring to healing ourselves as well as the land. Standing in silent reverence, kneeling in awe, dancing in delight—these are the pieces of pilgrimage that yield transformation and kinship that last for eternity.

A labyrinth is a kind of pilgrimage for those who can't—for whatever reason—travel. There are great canvas carpets with paintings of the courses of the labyrinth at Chartres that travel around, finding themselves in parish halls and community centers. Labyrinths are constructed with sand-weighted bags holding a tealight candle, which are especially inviting on a cool and misty night. Stones can be used for a more permanent structure in a side yard. And for those with mobility issues, there are table labyrinths that can be "walked" with a tracing finger.

There are several styles of labyrinth—the one in the basement of Chartres Cathedral is popular and the Cretan style is the simplest. In the labyrinth, the journey and the process are more important than the destination, after all. It is not a trick and a memory game, like a maze. It is a winding procession into the center of all that is, where there lie memories and revelations as well as reassurance that the thing—whatever the thing happens to be—is manageable. You do the labyrinth yourself, confident of both the going in and the coming out. We talked about the spiral of energy in the first part of this book and the labyrinth is that spiral made manifest, walkable, traceable.

Season's End

We wander into this place of mist and soil, of flood, and of the desire for things we can barely name because the culture we have lived in has lost it, sold it, and buried it. These markers in the cycle of the seasons give us pause and afford us a place to stop cosplaying life or pretending we are characters in our favorite tales, but instead engage in the lust and grief and joy that can be and are our birthright. When we honor the night season, the hollow hills, and all the places that integrate the spiritual into the physical, we can at last walk our spiritual talk. We can linger in this place of mystery and safety and know that we are one with All That Is, All That Was, and All That Will Be. We will stand in a place we have known only in dreams: we will be home at last.

Part Three

Hearth

Kindling, rekindling—this final section is a place to integrate some of the ideas we have explored in the other parts of this book. We will use the idea of the hearth—the hub of the house—as metaphor, seat of power, and launching pad for personal expression. We'll settle into the stage of moving animism, permaculture, acknowledged kinship, and our sojourn on the Wheel of the Agricultural Year as a form that we can pass on to others or integrate into our own and our family's personal practice. Together we will explore this spiritual and physical immersion into the seasons and their ceremonial markers, whether the reader finds herself on a farm in the country, a condo in the city, or any place in between. It is about the old-fashioned notion of homeliness and the act of kindling something like hope in the very heart of our woven world.

CHAPTER EIGHT

Homely

Homely: simple, cozy, and comfortable, as in one's own home;
unpretentious; plain or ordinary, but pleasant

Letter from the Kitchen Table: In Praise of Homeliness

I have been absorbed these many weeks in living this book as I was writing it. Every day finds me in the chair under the old apple tree, notebook in hand, observing, listening, dreaming. Days begin much as they end—in gratitude for the opportunity to be with this land that I love, in these gardens I have tended for all these years. Dishes washed and kitchen surfaces wiped down, the satisfying click of the electric kettle means there will soon be a cuppa of nettle tea and a shortbread cookie.

During the pandemic, I was able to stretch time to suit the needs of gardening, obligations as both friend and clergy, and handwriting a book on the reconnection of my Pagan communities with the Earth they claim to venerate. Through the fuddlement of various civic bodies, my goal has been to invite my friends to celebrate quite a homely life—a life simply and joyfully lived.

I have been sneaking nibbles of some of my comfort books: *Linnets and Valerians* by Elizabeth Goudge and Dylan Thomas's *A Child's Christmas in Wales*. You'd be quite right to suspect that the books of James Herriot might be the next in the stack. In spite of the primal concern I have for all of us now, it is the bliss of being in the land that brings me solace in these times—the land and the homeplace, the little forest-farm.

Real estate agents love to post advertisements for available rentals and sales with an invitation to buy a new "home." What a ridiculous notion—that a home can be bought. Homes are created; they are not for sale. Let's look at the notion of *home*: what it means, what it is, and how we deepen our kinship with the space in which we dwell.

As with the notion of intentional family, many of us grew up in spaces that weren't really homes, and it may require us to be out and on our own to understand the depth and breadth of the concept of home. We aren't thinking about homesteading, which is a very different thing. We aren't thinking about only residing only in stand-alone houses. Home can be anywhere we live, but it must have some of the following characteristics.

It must be as safe as you can make it. Some of us live in neighborhoods that are not particularly safe, and as a result, our living space is compromised. Safety is always relative, and none of us—none of this—is ever perfectly safe. We do the best we can with what we have, and then we make do. It has always been that way for us, for common people.

A home has the tangible pieces of the life you have lived. As we age, it sometimes seems we have lived several lives—sometimes interconnected, sometimes wildly separate. For those of us who have moved on from the religions and spiritual practices of our earliest years, there can be a sense of being reborn when we find the spiritual path that fits our feet, and the things we choose to have around us may hold pieces of that earlier time—the family Bible, photos from your First Communion—as well as pieces of the path you walk now.

A home should feel comfortable and be a place where you can behave as you please and don't have to put on the persona that your work life may require. It is a place where you should feel comfortable, with a chair that fits your body and dishes that give you pleasure to use.

Many of us would feel uncomfortable in the sorts of houses we see in magazines, which have few ornamentations and little furniture. Others of us are perfectly content in a simple place with less stuff to attend to. And there is every other permutation of how living space can be when it is tailored to the needs and wants of the people who inhabit it.

There is no one way that works for all people, and that is as it should be. Find the style that works for you and for your family—whether intentional or blood—and make the effort together to create it. Some people prefer Victorian mayhem while others are drawn to a Japanese-style simplicity. If you hate a mess but are choosing to live in one, then it is up to you to figure out why you are living in a style that keeps you on edge and shames you. Take the time—one surface here, one closet there—to create your little world of home. Work out the compromises, as best you can, with the people who share the space with you.

Your home is the place where it all comes together—the physical, the spiritual, the Descendants and the Ancestors, the spirit folk and the work-out machine. It is, as the samplers all imply, where the heart is. And for us, as we deepen our own intentional kinships and broaden our animism, it is the laboratory and crucible in which many things can be considered.

Join me for a cup of tea as we fold the physical and the spiritual into this odd and imperfect place we call home.

Kitchen as Living Space

No matter how much I tidy the rest of the house or how perfectly I have set out refreshments on the long dining room table, my guests inevitably end up cheek-by-jowl in my large kitchen. The table will be covered with glasses, bottles, and plates, and chairs will be rounded up from other rooms. At some point, the tastiest snack from the dining room will wander in with someone who can't stop eating the guacamole, and empty bottles will be cleared so that space is made on the kitchen table.

There is a closed-up fireplace against one wall, and I'd love to open it up again, though the cost is prohibitive. Nevertheless, it is the hearth in this home and proof that the idea of a hearth can be literal and meta-phorical. This hearth-room is a place where I cook, eat, and wash dishes. It is a place where food is stored as well as prepared. Garden produce lays on the drain board until it goes into the sink to be washed. I make medi-cine here, and magic, and jam. I make art on the kitchen table, and I write here, too. This room is the place where I sit with friends for counseling and comfort. It is where I watch my few TV shows and where I listen to NPR in the morning and the BBC at night. It's a big room for an old house—sixteen by sixteen—and it sees an awful lot of life.

It is the heart of this home, and the same is true for many of you. If this room can do so much, what other rooms in your house see the same cacophony of experiences? Have you rewritten the traditional theme of a room to make it fit your actual life? Do you really need a den? Maybe you need a craft room or an altar room or a place to store all the canned goods you've prepared for the Winter.

There is a delightful book from the 1970s called *Escarole in the Bed-room: Growing Food Plants Indoors* by Jack Kramer, one of the many offer-ings during the American passion for getting "back to the land." It is something worth considering if you have a room with a south-facing window. Grow lettuces in the bedroom window. Have a wall of books, if that comforts you. Set up a small table with an electric kettle, a teapot, a selection of teas, and a tin of cookies, just like that bed-and-breakfast place you stayed at in Dundee. If you love your work, as I do, have your work-desk there so you can leap out of bed and start writing something wild and wonderful.

But many people have trouble sleeping; if you do, consider what makes your sleeping-place feel calm, dark, and conducive to sleeping: low light, not too much furniture, beautiful sheets fresh from the clothes line, smelling of sun?

If your home is also home to other people, you may find that your bedroom then becomes your private space, your sanctuary. Set rules and boundaries for yourself and your home-mates about who can enter and when that entry may occur.

Inside to Outside: Porches, Stoops, Fire Escapes, and Decks

In former times, many people spent much of the day outside the house, working in field or factory. Creating and enjoying a place that is neither completely out nor completely in are one way to stretch your domestic space. As a rural child, the idea of a city stoop or—better yet—a fire escape on a brick apartment building was intriguing to me. I imagined the possibilities of sitting with friends and neighbors and watching the world go by. Our front door opened onto a small and rickety concrete slab with no overhang to shelter us as we came in or went out. There was once an overhanging roof and a porch underneath, but my mother said the roof shadowed the interior too much and had my father remove it. The kitchen door opened directly into a small side yard that separated the house from the woods. You stepped directly from the doorway onto the dirt of the yard.

All these almost-outdoor spaces create an opportunity for us to sit in either friendship or contemplation, enjoying a beverage or snack. They can be a place where we are not working or striving or achieving. They are a place where we have permission to simply be.

Home Altars, Inside and Out

Regardless of your spiritual tradition, you may find it comforting to set up an altar in your living space. Calling it an *altar* is a misnomer, of course, because altars are historically speaking a place where a sacrifice is conducted. But the word as it is commonly used is a place to remember our spiritual work and connections. There are as many sorts of altars as there are people who seek that spiritual anchor. Some friends' houses are full of altars, big and small, while others have a single one tucked away in a private, secluded place. As with all our discussions here, you must do the work of deciding what works for you and then put it into practice. You may also choose to set up an altar space outside under your favorite tree and near your firepit. It is obviously wise not to put precious breakable things on your outdoor altar. Select sturdy, weighty statuary and other tools, cloth coverings that don't mind getting wet and possibly pooped on, and candles in heavy holders. As we consider the role of animism in our burgeoning spirituality, recall how those moments of contemplation and journeying have been enhanced by your presence in the natural world, whether garden, porch, or urban fire escape.

Feeding Stations for the Dead, the Disembodied, and Even Birds

In addition to outdoor altars, you may also consider a place where offerings can be left for the Ancestors, the land spirits, and the Kindly Ones, as we discussed in Chapter 5. This can be a flat rock under a tree, the corner of a low wall—really anywhere you can leave a little food, drink, or other offerings. You may also be feeding birds, squirrels, mice, and other folk, and that is generous, too. We have a sleek fat rat who occasionally beds down in one of our compost barrels and looks up sleepily when we go to dump the bin from the kitchen.

Summer Kitchens

Another aspect of old homesteads was the use of a summer kitchen. These were areas outside the main house where cooking was done, sometimes by servants. An outdoor kitchen makes a focal point now for the making of medicines and for canning Summer's bounty. It can include a wood-fired oven made of brick and cob, which is perfect for baking bread and pizza. If you choose a wood-fired cook stove as well, you won't need any electricity run to your outdoor kitchen, and the preparation of these products will give you old skills, newly learned.

Cooking

As we discussed above, the heart of most homes is the kitchen, so I want to say a few words about cooking. Not the how-tos—there are thousands of books and websites about that—but the whys. Our sojourn in the COVID-19 pandemic time has reminded us that a surprising number of people don't cook for themselves at all and even more of us cook only on special occasions. We are reliant on grab-and-go convenience foods, fast food, and restaurants, either dining in or taking away. When those options were no longer possible during that shelter-at-home period, there was a mad scramble to remember the old ways, and many calls were made to mothers and grandmothers to ask about a particular family dish that was well-remembered and beloved.

Cooking can certainly be an art form, but the act itself of putting together a set of ingredients in a particular way in order to bring nutrition and comfort to oneself and one's kinfolk does not require art. It requires the resources to obtain the ingredients, the knowledge of how to put them together, and the time taken to prepare, cook, eat, and clean up afterwards. Like ironing and gardening, some of us will never have a passion for cooking, but for those who do, this homely act of community-building is a gift to those who partake in it. Created with some knowledge and much love, a cooked meal is an act of the greatest sanctity and love.

Table Setting

As we grow older, some of us inherit "mother's china," and that is becoming a burden for some. The old-fashioned patterns of the 1950s and '60s don't have much appeal anymore, and there are sad stories about the inability to sell or even give away those twenty-piece place settings of yesteryear. Bah. Setting a pretty table is no bad thing, though you may not need such an expansive service more than a few times a year. Setting a beautiful table tells your guests that you think enough of them to take the time to get out matching plates, to wash and iron cloth napkins, and to honor the gift of their presence. Hospitality, as I have said many times and written in many places, is the oldest spiritual obligation.

Tea Towels and Other Kitchen Cloths

Paper towels are a non-starter in my house—I use them only when I am draining bacon or wiping oil into a cast-iron pan. I probably don't use a roll of paper towels in a year. Instead we have a collection of tea towels and absorbent kitchen towels. They wipe up messes, dry our hands, make a place to drain glasses on the drain board, and line baskets of breads and cakes. I collect them on my travels but don't tuck them away in drawers after I get home. Every time I use that funny towel from Cornwall, it reminds me of my friends there and the day at Lands' End where I drank scrumpy, the native and very strong cider, for the first time. As a thrifter, I also buy linen dresses and skirts and cut them into tea towels, hemming them by hand and using them happily. Linen and good cotton get better and softer with age, and those lovely garments are things I would never wear.

Dishwashing

My daughter was quite smug when she moved into her apartment and informed me that she had a washer and dryer, a disposal, central air conditioning, and a dishwasher. As she was growing up, the only one of those things she had was a washing machine, which she learned to use at an early age. The rest was handled manually. The thing she was happiest about then—and still pleased about in her current place—is the dishwasher. I still don't know exactly how to work one, though I suspect I'd catch on pretty quickly if I had to. As I get older, though, I confess to enjoying the feel of hot water on my hands and the satisfaction of seeing the stacks of dishes lined up—clean and tidy—in the drying rack. And washing all those aforementioned dishes after a dinner party gives me the chance to wind down before bed.

Laundry as Meditative Practice

Since we are on the subject of laundry, let's look at it for a moment only. Most of us do this with little thought, as it is a necessary chore that is repetitive and not particularly satisfying. With the advent of household appliances, women—who did and still do the bulk of domestic labor—were assured that these machines would lead to more leisure. They were advertised as time-saving devices. What we discovered is that, if we let it, work will expand to fit whatever amount of time is on offer. Soon after the average home had a washing machine, a dishwasher, a clothes dryer, and all the others, women joined the workforce in greater numbers and so had work outside the home—paid work—in addition to the now "easier" chores inside the home. It is now common to put the laundry in to wash and after half an hour to move it to the dryer. Then it is taken out—possibly sorted, possibly folded—and taken to its various drawers and closets. Out of sight, out of mind. We wash clothes that have been lightly worn and aren't really dirty. We don't think much about the process of cleaning, of washing: we are grateful when we can afford an energy- and water-saving machine, and we sigh about the endless laundry.

For a moment, let's think about the old idea of laundry day. One day a week was set aside, and water was boiled and washing was done. It took most of the day because the clean clothes and household linens were hung to dry, either on a line in the sun or on designated racks in the house.

Drying Racks and Clothes Lines

Our clothes dryer gave up the ghost during the diaper years, and we simply didn't replace it. Some people are astounded with the thought that we live happily without that appliance, but the truth is, if it's sunny outside, the clothes go on a clothes line and, if the weather is inclement, they go on a rack in the house over a furnace vent. I do not have a large family, to be honest, and the amount of laundry for many children might have been overwhelming. But this worked for our small family and continues to work well, with my daughter in her own place with her dryer, dishwasher, and air conditioning.

Ironing

This is an acquired taste, I suspect, and there are many people who never acquire it. Ironing appeals to my craving for instant gratification—clean but wrinkled linens are sprinkled with water and left to rest for a brief time. The iron is heated to steaming, and one by one, each piece is evened out by hand then pressed with heat and steam, a process from which it emerges flat and smooth. Then it is folded in the desired shape and put away in a basket or drawer for future use.

Few garments these days require ironing, and some that do look fine without it. I limit my ironing to sewing projects, table linens, and cotton handkerchiefs. When I lived with my grandmother, she owned a looming appliance she referred to as the ironer—it was a clothes press, the kind that is sometimes called a mangle. She sat in the little metal chair that came with it and ironed the cotton bed sheets that were her pride and joy. It was operated with a foot pedal that raised and lowered the cloth-covered roller. I never got the knack of using it but liked to watch her operate the machine.

I use a vintage wooden ironing board with a thick pad. My preference is for a heavy iron because the heavier the iron, the less work for the ironer. But most now are lightweight, which may be the reason so many people hate to iron.

Aprons

Aprons are handy. You would be wise to have an assortment of aprons for all your projects and chores—a heavy canvas one with big pockets for the garden, several lighter ones for the kitchen, a really pretty one that stays clean and is only for show, a vintage one that makes you smile. One of the legacies of my great-grandmother was the story of her apron. She always wore one—most women did in those days because laundry was never an easy thing and they did not have unlimited changes of clothing as most of us do today. She always had on an apron, and it was always dirty. She had many children and ran a neighborhood grocery store as well as her household—which were in the same building—so a well-used apron is hardly a surprise. The joke was that when someone came over to the house or at the beginning of the day in the store, the apron was carefully turned over—and the underside was always as stained as the front.

I have working aprons and then aprons that just hang on the door into the pantry. I find aprons for friends and love to receive aprons in return. Unlike my great-grandmother, however, my aprons are clean, if stained. That's probably because I have a washing machine and don't have to heat water on the stove, use a washboard in a tin pan of soapy water, roll the wash through the wringer, rinse, and repeat.

Thrifting and Swaps

The road calls me for most of the year—especially during festival and conference season—and that gives me an excuse to check out thrift stores in all sorts of places. There is so much you can learn about a community by both the quantity and quality of its thrift stores. When I am home, there are several that I check out, usually a few times a month. Since I am not doing resale, I have specific sorts of items that I look for. This saves me time, of course, but it also means I don't give the entire shop more than a cursory glance and miss the treats that are hiding in the back of a shelf. As you might guess from my love of tea towels, linens are one of the items I seek out. Embroidered pillow cases made of soft and often-laundered Egyptian cotton are a favorite, as well as any table linen with hand-tatted or crocheted edging. Because I can't seem to help myself, I always spend time with the crystal and glassware section where I have gotten Waterford crystal bowls for a song and a set of matching wine glasses of no particular pedigree for fifty cents apiece. You won't be bothered if someone breaks such a wine glass, and you also won't mind replacing the whole set when you find some in a better size or better quality during your thrifting expeditions. This assumes you enjoy this activity, and some people don't. It is silly to do things you detest because someone else finds it pleasurable. Unless, of course, your friend invites you thrifting in exchange for her playing mini-golf with you—that's a case of sharing something with someone you love and enjoying the activity because of the company.

Periodically a group of friends will decide to hold a swap where we all bring clothing we no longer want and lay it on blankets on the floor, and everyone goes through all the clothes and selects the things they can use. There is usually a potluck attached to these gatherings, and they function as a social event as well as a chance to offload those things that don't fit—and maybe never did fit but you kept just in case. New mothers often band together for swaps because children outgrow clothes so quickly. Money doesn't change hands, and someone is designated to take all the things left behind to a local charity shop.

Conclusion

We have taken a tour of some of the rooms that collect our lives and hold them close, places where can savor what we have and what we do and who we are. Not everyone has rooms, and we should remember that. Not everyone lives in the way that we do, whatever way that is. The awareness of that should bring us a sense of curiosity about others as well as awaken in us—if it was not awakened before—a sense of the importance of the ancient blessing of hospitality.

There is so much to do, every day, to tuck in the ends of this weaving we are creating: to observe and really see, to listen and really hear, to integrate our intuition and our Ancestral memory into a practice so practiced it no longer feels artificial. It only feels like living a good life and a full one.

Glossary

acknowledged and intentional kinship: the humble and necessary act of claiming one's place in the webs of being

animism: the belief that all parts of the earth and the land itself have souls

Anthropocene: the geological age in which human activity is the dominant influence on the planet

boundaries: the lines that delineate a particular space; the emotional boundaries that humans set around their personal and energetic space

circles on the ground: localized organizational structures that can most swiftly meet the needs of people and planet

Cross-Quarter Day: the days midway between the Solstices and Equinoxes, i.e., the Quarter Days that divide up the ceremonial and agricultural year; with the Cross-Quarter Days, the year is made up of eight parts

Ember Days: in the Christian church, three days in each season set aside for fasting, abstinence, and prayer; reclaimed and repurposed in land-based spiritualities as a time to renew commitment to life and to reinvigorate spiritual practice. Spring Embertide is the first week of March and dedicated to planting. Summer Embertide is the second week in June and dedicated to a bountiful harvest. Autumn Embertide is the third week in September and dedicated to the work and products of vintners, brewers, and cider makers. Winter Embertide is the second week in December and dedicated to collecting and storing seeds for the following agricultural year.

Gabbleratchet: an old term for flights of wild geese

hearing: the act of observing sound, whether birdsong or music, human speech or waterfall; a spiritual act of devotion

holey stones: stones with naturally occurring holes that pierce all the way through the rock

hollow hills: the mythical homes of spirit beings and Ancestors; also, burial mounds

home: a place that can be physical, imaginary, or symbolic in which one may dwell in peace and comfort

homely: plain, cozy, and comfortable; unpretentious

Listening for the Hoofbeat of God: an accidental corruption of John Philip Newell's book of Celtic Christian spirituality *Listening for the Heartbeat of God*

Martinmas: originally the feast day of St. Martin of Tours; also a folkloric holiday that marks the end of the final harvest

Michaelmas: originally the feast day of the Archangel Michael specifically and all the archangels generally; in folk history it is the end of the farmers' year and celebrated with feasting and games

perennial: a plant that regrows from its roots after the dormancy of Winter

permaculture: a holistic philosophy of permanent agriculture coupled with a permanent worldview of respect for the natural world

processions: parades, large or small, with a specific intention

pruning/deadwood: pruning is the act of trimming a plant, either to remove dead limbs (deadwood) or to give it a desired shape

Quarter Days: the two Solstices and two Equinoxes

Rogation Day: a Pagan Roman holdover that the Christian Church absorbed, it was a time (April 25) set aside for fasting and prayer; the Roman celebration included processions from the urban center into the countryside to make special sacrifice and prayers to insure a bountiful harvest; repurposed here as a time for Earth-honoring people to acknowledge their powerlessness in the face of weather systems and other examples of planetary power

seeing: the act of observing life visually, whether sunset or new lamb, an elder's hands or a prairie; a spiritual act of devotion

spinning: the act of making cleaned and combed animal fur into yarn

vigil: a period of keeping awake or otherwise focused on a particular prayerful intention

webs of living: the nodes of kinship and biological function into which the whole of the planet is organized; these are seen as interactive and responsive, both within the individual web and throughout the connected structures

Resources

Books

Angier, Bradford. *One Acre and Security: How to Live off the Earth without Ruining It.* Mechanicsburg, PA: Stackpole Books, 2017.

Beckett, Barbara. *The Country Kitchen: Chutneys and Pickles.* Lincolnton, UK: Harlaxton Publishing Ltd., 1993.

Bede. *The Reckoning of Time (De temporum ratione).* Faith Wallis, trans., Liverpool, UK: Liverpool University Press, 1999.

Blackie, Dr. Sharon. *If Women Rose Rooted.* London: September Publishing, 2016.

Buhner, Stephen. *Sacred and Herbal Healing Beers.* Boulder, CO: Siris Books: 1998.

Crawford, Martin. *Creating a Forest Garden: Working with Nature to Grow Edible Crops.* Cambridge, UK: Green Books, 2010.

Dames, Michael. *The Silbury Treasure.* London: Thames and Hudson Ltd., 1976.

Endicott, Gwendolyn. *The Spinning Wheel: The Art of Mythmaking.* Attic Press, 1994.

English, Ashley. *Canning and Preserving: All You Need to Know to Make Jams, Jellies, Pickles, Chutneys and More.* Asheville, NC: Lark Books, 2010.

————. *Essential Book of Homesteading: All You Need to Know about Homemade Living.* Asheville, NC: Lark Books, 2017.

Feher-Elston, Catherine. *Ravensong: A Natural and Fabulous History of Ravens and Crows.* New York: TarcherPerigee, 2005.

Flottum, Kim. *The Backyard Beekeeper.* Beverly, MA: Quarry Books, 2018.

Goudge, Elizabeth. *Linnets and Valerians.* Reprint: Boston: David Godine, 2015.

Gray, Nicholas Stuart. *The Apple Stone.* Reprint: New York: Meredith Press, 1969.

Hardy, Thomas. *Under the Greenwood Tree.* Reprint: Oxford University Press, 1999.

Hartley, Dorothy. *Lost Country Life.* Reprint: New York: Pantheon Books, 1979.

Homans, George C. *English Villagers of the Thirteenth Century.* New York: Norton and Co., 1975.

Hughes, Nathaniel. *Weeds in the Heart: The Practice of Intuitive Herbalism.* London: Aeon Books Ltd., 2018.

Jensen, Derrick. *A Language Older than Words.* White River Junction, VT: Chelsea Green Publishing, 2004.

———. *Listening to the Land.* White River Junction, VT: Chelsea Green Publishing, 2008.

Kains, M. G. *Five Acres and Independence.* New York: Pocket Books, 1948.

Katz, Sandor. *The Art of Fermentation.* White River Junction, VT: Chelsea Green, 2012.

Kindred, Glennie. *Earth Wisdom.* Carlsbad, CA: Hay House, 2004.

———. *Letting in the Wild Edges.* Hampshire, UK: Permanent Publications, 2013.

Kramer, Jack. *Escarole in the Bedroom: Growing Food Plants Indoors.* New York: Little, Brown, 1977.

Linebaugh, Peter. *The Incomplete True, Authentic, and Wonderful History of May Day.* Oakland, CA: PM Press, 2016.

Louv, Richard. *Last Child in the Woods.* New York: Workman Publishing Company, 2005.

———. *Our Wild Calling.* New York: Workman Publishing Company, 2019.

Lovelock, James. *Gaia: A New Look at Life on Earth.* Oxford University Press, 2000.

———. *The Revenge of Gaia.* New York: Perseus Books Group, 2006.

Macy, Joanna, and John Seed. *Thinking like a Mountain.* Philadelphia, PA: New Society Publishers, 1988.

Nichols, Beverley. *Down the Garden Path.* Reprint: Portland, OR: Timber Press, 2004.

Pollan, Michael. *The Botany of Desire.* New York: Penguin Random House: 2001.

———. *In Defense of Food: An Eater's Manifesto.* New York: Penguin Press, 2008.

Meyenberg, Albert. *Homiletic and Catechetic Studies.* New York: F. Pustet and Company, 1912.

Shaw, Martin. *Scatterlings: Getting Claimed in the Age of Amnesia.* Ashland, OR: White Cloud Press, 2016.

Shehan, Amber. *Artisanal Small-Batch Brewing.* Salem, MA: Page Street Publishing Co., 2019.

Smith, Chris. *The Whole Okra: A Seed to Stem Celebration.* White River Junction, VT: Chelsea Green Publishing, 2019.

Stamets, Paul. *Mycelium Running.* Berkeley, CA: Ten Speed Press, 2005.

Starhawk. *The Earth Path.* San Francisco: HarperSanFrancisco, 2004.

———. *The Empowerment Manual: A Guide for Collaborative Groups.* Gabriola Island, BC: New Society Publishers, 2011.

Stewart, Amy. *The Earth Moved: On the Remarkable Achievements of Earthworms.* Chapel Hill, NC: Algonquin Books, 2004.

Strauss, Paul. *The Big Herbs.* Gambier, OH: XOXOX Press, 2014.

Thomas, Dylan. *A Child's Christmas in Wales.*

Weber, Andreas. *Matter and Desire: An Erotic Ecology.* White River Junction, VT: Chelsea Green Publishing, 2017.

Wise, William H. *The Wise Encyclopedia of Cookery.* New York: Wm. H. Wise and Co., Inc., 1949.

Other Resources

Arbor Day, *arborday.org*

BeLoved Asheville, *belovedasheville.com*

Earth Day, *earth.org*

Equinox Farm and Equinox Botanicals, *equinoxbotanicals.com*

Findhorn Ecovillage, *ecovillagefindhorn.com*

Incredible Edible Todmorden Ltd., *incredibledible-todmorden.co.uk*

Low Country Blessing Box Project, *chsblessingbox.org*

Organic Growers School, *organicgrowersschool.org*

Sow True Seed, *sowtrueseed.com*

United Plant Savers, *unitedplantsavers.org*

About the Author

Byron Ballard has called western North Carolina home since her birth at the local Seventh Day Adventist TB sanitarium. Her education includes a Bachelor of Arts in theater and a Master of Fine Arts in the same field. She studies and practices Appalachian folk magic, a traditional folkway that she's dubbed "hillfolks' hoodoo." Her research into its origins has led her to fieldwork throughout the British Isles. Her books on the subject include *Staubs and Ditchwater: A Friendly and Useful Introduction to Hillfolks' Hoodoo* (Silver Rings Press, 2012), *Asfidity and Mad-Stones* (Smith Bridge Press, 2014), and *Roots, Branches, and Spirits: The Folkways and Witchery of Appalachia* (Llewellyn International, 2021). *Embracing Willendorf: A Witch's Way of Loving Your Body to Health and Fitness* (Smith Bridge Press) debuted in 2017 and *Earth Works: Ceremonies in Tower Time* (Smith Bridge Press) was released in 2018. She is currently working on *The Ragged Wound: Tending the Soul of Appalachia* for Smith Bridge Press.

She has served as a featured speaker and teacher at festivals and conferences that include Sacred Space Conference, Heartland, Sirius Rising, Starwood, FaerieCon, Pagan Spirit Gathering, Southeast Wise Women's Herbal Conference, Glastonbury Goddess Conference, the Scottish Pagan Federation Conference, and Mystic South Conference. A member of the Appalachian Studies Association, she recently presented the paper "The Ragged Wound," which has become the core of her current work in progress.

Byron serves as senior priestess and cofounder of Mother Grove Goddess Temple in Asheville. She is also one of the founders of the Coalition of Earth Religions/CERES, a Pagan nonprofit, and she does interfaith work locally and regionally.

She is a folklorist, playwright, gardener, and a tai chi student who blogs irregularly and talks about Tower Time far too often. You can find her at her website *www.myvillagewitch.com* and on Facebook, Instagram, and Twitter.